SMOOTH SAILING INTO RETIREMENT

How to Navigate the Transition from Work to Leisure

By Dave Hughes

Prickly Pair Publishing
Chandler, Arizona, USA

Visit www.retireFabulously.com to discover more valuable resources and informative articles about retirement lifestyle planning.

If you would like to contact the author, please send email to SSIR-book@retirefabulously.com.

Editor: Mark McNease
Cover photo: James Royce
Cover design: Dave Hughes

Portions of this content have previously appeared on my website, RetireFabulously.com and/or my blog on U.S. News.com.

Library of Congress Control Number: 2017962208

ISBN-13: 978-0-9970017-2-3
ISBN-10: 0997001720

Table of Contents

Gratitude

I would like to express my sincere gratitude to:

Mark McNease, creator, editor and publisher of lgbtSr.org for his unwavering support, encouragement and great advice. Mark is a successful author in his own right, having published a series of mystery novels and anthologies. He did an excellent job as the editor of this book. Please visit MarkMcNease.com to discover Mark's work.

Emily Brandon, senior editor of the Retirement blogs at U.S. News & World Report, for allowing me the opportunity to contribute articles to U.S. News.

Everyone who subscribes to the *Retire Fabulously!* website or follows the *Retire Fabulously!* page on Facebook. Many of my readers have provided thoughtful comments and participated in my surveys. You make doing all of this worthwhile.

Most of all, my husband, Jeff McKeehan, for his constant support, his valuable feedback, and his efforts to help promote *Retire Fabulously!* Jeff endures, without complaint, the long hours I have spent working on my website and this book that I could be spending with him and the dogs. Every spouse of a writer will understand exactly what I'm talking about.

PART ONE

Your Last Few Months of Work

Chapter 1

5 Reasons You Shouldn't Wait Until You Retire to Figure Out What You're Going to Do

"Don't simply retire from something; have something to retire to."
- Harry Emerson Fosdick

When you were five, ten, or even twenty years away from retiring, what you would do after you retire was probably the farthest thing from your mind. You were busy and had your career to focus on. If you had kids at home, it was all you could do to keep track of their activities and needs.

Even with less than a year to go, you may be unsure of what to expect the day after you leave your workplace for the last time. Perhaps you are dreading retirement and you would rather not think about being retired until the time comes. Why should this be complicated? You simply stop going into work each day. What's the big deal?

As you'll learn in this book, it's actually a very big deal. Many parts of your life will suddenly be different once you no longer have your job.

It's wise to start planning what you're going to do on a day-to-day basis before that time actually comes. Here are five reasons why you shouldn't wait until you retire to figure out what you're going to do with your life after you end your career.

1. If you're going to start a business, there are many things you can do before you leave work.

Many retirees start their own businesses after they retire, either because they need the money or because it's something they want to do. For the past several years, the highest rate of entrepreneurial activity has occurred among people aged 55-64. Your business can be consulting, selling art or crafts, running a flea market booth, training, speaking, freelance writing, or just about anything you can imagine.

Most businesses take a couple years to ramp up. Before you leave work, you can develop contacts, get training or certifications you may need, and start developing your business during your evenings and weekends. Then when the big day comes, you can hit the ground running.

2. You may be forced to retire sooner than you plan to.

On average, people retire three years earlier than planned. While many people consider the standard retirement age to be 65, today the average retirement age is actually 62.

Early retirement could be precipitated by an injury or illness, an attractive early retirement package, or a layoff. Perhaps you'll need to retire early to take care of your spouse or a parent. Regardless of the circumstances, if you assume that you still have a few more years to think about how you'll spend your retirement days, you will be unprepared if retirement comes sooner than expected.

3. It gives you something concrete to look forward to.

Most Americans are financially under-prepared for retirement. There are many possible reasons, but one reason is that people have little motivation to save when they don't know what they are saving for.

Having dreams and goals for the future gives you direction, hope, and optimism. If you can create a clear vision for how you want to live after you retire, you will have a better idea of how much money you will need to have saved in order to enjoy the retirement lifestyle you envision.

4. It allows you to create a more realistic retirement budget and determine whether you're saving enough.

The amount of money you'll need is highly variable and dependent upon the lifestyle you wish to enjoy after you retire.

Do you want to continue to live in your current house or downsize to something smaller?

Do you plan to move to an area where the cost of living is higher or lower than where you live now?

How much traveling do you want to do, and what kind of travel?

Are you willing to seek out senior discounts and live as frugally as possible?

Can you change your shopping and dining habits?

What hobbies and recreational activities do you plan to engage in?

The answers to these and many other questions will determine how much money you'll need after you retire.

Some people find it helpful to try living on their anticipated retirement budget for a year while they are still working. You won't be able to completely simulate your anticipated retirement experience – for example, you'll still incur the cost of commuting to work and you may not be able to travel as much as you hope to after you retire. But this exercise should give you a good indication of whether or not your retirement budget is realistic.

5. It might be easier to buy your retirement home while you still have a working income.

Once you quit your job, it may be harder to qualify for a mortgage or receive approval for other forms of financing and credit. You'll almost certainly have a reduced level of income.

Similarly, if you plan to tour the country in a recreational vehicle or buy a boat, those things might be easier to buy while you're working.

*****

While it's important to live in the present, it's also important to have some idea where you're heading. It's good to have things to look forward to. By visualizing and defining what your life will be like after you retire, you will be able to lay some of the groundwork to ensure that you can enjoy the retirement lifestyle you want when the time comes.

Chapter 2

How Things Will Change at Work after You Announce Your Retirement

"If hard work were such a wonderful thing,
surely the rich would have kept it all to themselves."
- Lane Kirkland

After decades of work, the blessed day you've been anticipating for years is finally visible on the horizon - your retirement date!

As the last few months pass and the countdown clock you probably have on your computer desktop ticks down the remaining days (and hours, minutes, and seconds), you will be eager to inform your boss of your plans and start spreading the news among your colleagues.

Whoa! Not so fast.

Before you start shouting your good news from the rooftop, you should carefully consider the timing of your big announcement.

You should give your manager a reasonable amount of notice, just as you would if you were simply resigning to take another job. Two weeks is customary, but depending on the nature of your position it may be appropriate for you to give longer notice if it will take time to hire your replacement and train him or her. Generally, if you're a higher-level employee or your position and skills are unique and not easily transferable to others, then giving more advance notice is appropriate.

If your company has a policy for how far in advance you should submit your resignation, then by all means, follow that policy. You should also investigate whether your company has separate guidelines for announcing your retirement and learn what they are.

Once you have considered all of this, I strongly recommend that you give notice no farther in advance than you need to.

Why? Because as soon as you announce your retirement, your work life will probably change drastically.

Your manager won't want to assign you to a project that has a completion date beyond your retirement date, and that's reasonable. But people are likely to assume that you aren't interested in doing any more meaningful work. You'll be labeled a "short-timer."

In many ways, you'll be treated as if you're already gone.

Perhaps that won't bother you. You might be happy coasting for the last few weeks or months. But if your work ethic is such that you desire to be productive and contribute until the end, you might be in for a disheartening experience.

Depending on how your company systematically treats departing people, you may simply be paid for your remaining time and told to not bother showing up. Worse, you could be told to stop showing up and not get paid.

I announced my retirement five months before my last day. I had every intention of working right up until the end. I wanted to continue to contribute to my company and earn my pay. I didn't want people's parting memory of me to be that I was a lazy slacker.

Within a week, the people who reported to me were re-assigned to someone else. I was given a few superfluous make-work assignments here and there for the rest of the five months. On most days, I had little of value to do.

For some people, several weeks or months of light work might be fine. It wasn't what I wanted, and nobody asked.

In addition to depriving the company of value that they were paying for, it was demeaning. It left me with the message that I was no longer valued and I could be quickly and easily cast aside. This treatment was not an indication of my performance. In fact, I regularly received excellent performance reviews, I had been recently promoted, and I was widely regarded as one of the best managers in the organization.

So wait as long as you can to give notice of your retirement.

Not everybody will be as enthusiastic about your big announcement as you are.

Chapter 3

What if Your Company Retires You?

"There are so many other interesting ways to spend your time. I feel like early retirement is a gift, but it's such an incredible gift. It's a gift I need to use."
- Martha Felt-Bardon

It's no secret that the Baby Boomer generation (those born between 1946 and 1964) is now reaching retirement age.

Many companies are finding themselves top-heavy with gray-haired people in higher pay grades. The financial analysts are giving the top brass the message that it's time to thin the herd. For each person in their 50s or 60s they can somehow get rid of, they could hire two fresh, eager college graduates who have more current technical skills and who will be more willing to work 50 or 60 hours a week. (Never mind that the top brass are probably Baby Boomers themselves who, of course, receive the largest salaries.)

Simply firing people because they are too old is illegal, but there are other ways. The most popular method is the early retirement package. While the package is voluntary and you can choose whether or not to take it, the package is sometimes offered with the veiled hint that you would be well advised to take it.

It's as if you are being told, "Here, let me help you pack up your office. I'll hold the door open for you!"

If you find yourself retired a little sooner than you had planned, you may not be quite as prepared as you would have been if you had retired on your own timetable, in both practical and emotional ways. This chapter will help you with your transition.

Feelings

If you are retired by your company, you may feel bitterness and resentment. That's perfectly understandable. After years of hearing messages like "our people are our greatest assets" and "we want to help you reach your career goals," it's difficult to hear the song change to "thank you for your service. We won't be needing you anymore."

This situation is similar to going through a break-up or the loss of a loved one. It's healthy and normal to grieve for a while and let your emotions run their course. But then you need to pick yourself up and move on. Harboring prolonged anger will only make you miserable.

It's hard to go through the experience as it happens, but sooner or later you realize that things are alright again, and that new job you've found or that new partner you've met is better than the previous one. You realize that you're better off now than you were before.

Whether that realization occurs sooner or later is largely up to you. As unfair as it might have been for your company to lay you off or retire you early, it's your responsibility to deal with it and make the best of it. You can't control everything that happens to you in life, but you have control of how you respond to it and how you move forward. You can choose to look at this in terms of the new opportunities it is opening up for you. You have more options than you may realize, some of which I'll cover below.

Financial setback

The worst aspect of beginning your retirement sooner than expected is the financial impact. It's a triple-whammy. Your income stops, you have to start living off of your savings sooner, and if you're under 65, you may have to buy your own health insurance.

How you respond to this situation is largely dependent upon your personal circumstances.

If your savings are sufficient to pay the bills and cover your needs for daily living, you may simply accept that you won't be doing as much traveling as you had hoped or having as much discretionary income to spend. While having more money to spend during your retirement would have been nice, you can still have a happy retirement. There are many fun and fulfilling things to do that don't require a lot of money, and a good social life helps a lot. Once your basic needs are met, then having a higher level of discretionary income doesn't necessarily correlate to a higher level of happiness.

Finding another job

If your savings are not sufficient to pay the bills, or if you are younger than 59 1/2 and don't have access to your retirement accounts without paying an early withdrawal penalty, then you're going to have to consider ways to bring in some more money.

If it's any consolation, you're not alone. As many as 72% of all people in the U.S. expect that they will work in one way or another after they retire. They may be driven by financial necessity, the need to feel productive or relieve boredom, or the desire to do something they're totally passionate about.

You may have a hard time finding a job that is comparable to your last job, especially in terms of pay. You can try anyway, but be prepared for a difficult, lengthy, and frustrating job search.

Utilize your network as much as you can, and definitely have a plan B.

You may have to swallow your pride and take a job that pays significantly less than you have been accustomed to making. If you can find a job that provides health insurance benefits, so much the better.

Some retired Baby Boomers (as well as some pre-retirees) take matters into their own hands and become entrepreneurs. The only drawback to an entrepreneurial pursuit is that it takes time and often money to launch the business and it may be months or even years before you earn income.

Here are just a few options for retirement work. Some involve temporary employment, while others are more entrepreneurial. There are many other possibilities, but these examples should start the ideas flowing and expand your range of possibilities.

- Catering bartender or server
- Tour guide or museum docent
- Seasonal park worker
- Mail order fulfillment
- Seasonal retail employment
- Pet sitter or dog walker
- Handyman or repair service
- Holiday decorating or gift buying
- Party planner or wedding planner
- Author or freelance writer
- Photographer
- Antique or flea market vendor

You may be able to find a job that allows you to engage in activities that indulge your passions and takes advantage of your abilities.

Chapter 4

Your Retirement Party

"Celebrate endings, for they precede new beginnings."
- Jonathan Lockwood Huie

When you retire, you will probably have a party thrown for you. Commemorating the end of your decades-long career, honoring your career accomplishments, and bidding farewell to your colleagues are excellent reasons for a celebration!

You may get one retirement party from your workplace and another from your family and friends!

If your retirement party will not be planned by others, then plan it yourself! You owe yourself a celebration for this momentous occasion. It's one of the most significant milestones of your life.

This chapter contains valuable advice for how to plan and execute a memorable retirement party that will be a proper commemoration of a long career full of accomplishments as well as being fun for everyone.

There are several options for celebrating a retirement. Factors that enter into the planning decisions include budget, how many people you wish to invite, how easy it will be for them to attend, how much of a program or ceremony you wish to have, and whether or not you wish to serve alcohol.

The greatest consideration should be what the retiree wants.

For a retirement party thrown by your company for you that will be attended by your co-workers, a lunchtime event is usually the best option.

The advantages of a retirement lunch held at the workplace are that it's easy for people to attend, you will probably have the use of a projector and sound system if you want them, and you won't have non-guests nearby as you would if you held the party in a restaurant. A restaurant lunch is a viable option, especially if the restaurant has a separate dining room that can be reserved for your party.

The disadvantages are that you can't serve alcohol (unless company policy allows it), people may be limited on time or have work conflicts, and you won't be able to invite other people beyond your spouse and perhaps a few former co-workers from the same company. You'll have to provide for non-employee guests to be signed in to the premises and escorted (again, depending on company policy).

If you're planning a retirement party, it's essential to ask the retiree what type of party he or she wants and who he or she would like to invite. This is *NOT* an occasion for a surprise party! This is a once-in-a-lifetime event, and the guest of honor should have the kind of party he or she wants.

There are pros and cons to inviting a lot of people to your retirement party. Of course, budget considerations may inform how many people can be invited.

Generally, it's better to err on the side of inviting people who may not choose to come rather than not inviting people who would like to attend.

The biggest drawback to inviting a larger number of people is that the retiree will have a smaller amount of time to spend with each person. Most people will want to congratulate the guest of honor and spend a few minutes recalling good times, expressing appreciation, or talking about his or her plans for the future. If too many people are invited, some may feel that they didn't get enough time with the retiring coworker.

Pictures make a wonderful addition to a retirement party.

If the party will be in a room where a projector and a screen or plain white wall will be available, you can have a slide show running throughout the event, except during the program. If the room isn't conducive to a slide show, you can make several large posters with photo montages and place them around the room.

If there aren't many pictures available of the person in work-related settings, it's fine to include pictures from the person's personal life as long as they aren't embarrassing and don't infringe on the person's privacy. For example, you should avoid pictures of the person wearing a swim suit that may be too revealing or pictures of the person drunk at a stripper bar.

Childhood pictures will probably go over well, especially high school pictures with funny hairstyles and out-of-style clothing.

If your retirement party is going to include a period of time in which people who worked with the retiree will get a chance to speak, it's a good idea to have a Master of Ceremonies (MC). Hopefully, someone in your circle of acquaintances is a good fit for this role. Someone who belongs to a local Toastmasters club or has other public speaking experience would be a good choice.

Speakers should be solicited and confirmed ahead of time, and should be given the direction that their speech should last no longer than three to five minutes. The more speakers you have, the less time each should be allotted.

It is important to insist that speakers keep their remarks brief. Nothing will throw a wet rag over the party like someone talking too long.

You should decide whether or not to have a brief period for open mic. This is a risky proposition, especially if there is alcohol being served at your event. The MC should make it clear to people who come up for open mic that they should keep their remarks brief, and the MC should be ready to step in and thank the speaker (a polite way to cut him or her off) if their remarks are inappropriate or go on too long.

Humor is an essential ingredient for a retirement party.

A retirement party should be an uplifting, fun occasion. The best speeches are those that recall good times or funny incidents, as long as they aren't embarrassing. Brief expressions of gratitude or heartfelt appreciation are fine, but too much gushing over the retiree becomes trite and repetitive after a while.

Don't bother looking on the internet for retirement jokes. Most jokes are simply not funny, and some are mean-spirited, dirty, or otherwise inappropriate.

Any jokes or attempts at humor that are embarrassing, crass, or mean-spirited have no place whatsoever at a retirement party.

It's OK to gently poke fun of the person, especially if their personality characteristics and foibles are well-known and embraced by the honoree. It should be clear to everyone that the remarks are coming from a place of love and good humor.

This is not the place to air grudges or grind axes. The old adage, "if you can't say something nice, don't say anything at all" most certainly applies to retirement parties. Those who are selected to speak at the event should be coached accordingly.

Of course, the retiree should have the opportunity to speak, and he or she should probably be scheduled last on the agenda. While the retiree will probably have plenty of things to say, it's best to keep his or her remarks to ten minutes or less.

If you are the retiree, focus on a few key memories and keep your remarks light and humorous.

Your audience will not be interested in hearing a full run-down of your career and all the awards you received. Droning on for a long time will dampen the party and have people heading for the door. While it's true that this is your day and you are the person being honored, you don't want to cap off your career by boring people and leaving that as their lasting impression of you.

Have a good photographer on hand, and perhaps a videographer.

You probably have a friend or coworker who is a good photographer. He or she will probably be pleased to contribute to the retirement celebration. The resulting pictures will be well-composed and show people at their best. The photographer should try to capture everyone in the room in at least one photo. This special occasion should not be left to one or two well-meaning amateurs with their cell phone cameras.

Another option is to offer attendees the opportunity to submit photos or a handwritten note ahead of time. These can be compiled into a scrapbook and given to the honoree at the event. They can also be part of the slideshow that is shown as people arrive and eat.

Another idea is to set up a web site which contains a brief overview of the retiree's career and plans for the future, and provides a place where people can write well-wishes and tributes to the retiree.

In summary, a retirement party should be a fun, celebratory, memorable affair. It will come off best if it is thoughtfully planned by a team of several people. They should ask the retiree what he or she wants, and make every reasonable effort to accommodate those wishes.

If you are the retiree, don't be bashful about letting your planners know what you want, but stop short of meddling or micromanaging. The planning team may come up with some brilliant ideas that you never thought of!

PART TWO

Your First Few Months of Retirement

Chapter 5

Congratulations! You're Retired! ... Now What?

"Retirement means doing whatever I want to do.
It means choice."
- Dianne Nahirmy

You have probably been anticipating your retirement for many years. Perhaps you've entertained some general ideas about what your retirement will look like, but you're not sure what your day-to-day life will be like once the big day comes to pass.

Despite your years of anticipation, you may be surprised when you experience what it's really like to wake up and have no job to go to. You will find that your life will suddenly be different in more ways than you might ever have anticipated.

It's OK to let yourself chill out - for a little while.

For the first few weeks, it's fine to allow yourself time to decompress. You've earned it. If you despise your alarm clock, leave it off and get up whenever you like.

Do whatever you feel like doing each day.

Treat yourself to a movie or binge-watch some TV series on Hulu, Netflix, or Amazon Prime.

Read a book you've wanted to read.

Go for a drive or take a short getaway vacation in the middle of the week.

Stay up late.

Have a drink at 3:00 in the afternoon.

Book a spa day.

Indulge yourself. Be a little lazy. Do whatever you feel like doing - or do nothing.

That will feel great for a little while, but eventually you will come to the realization that this isn't sustainable. You will probably have at least another twenty or thirty years ahead of you and it won't be all carefree hedonism.

After you have allowed yourself a short period of time to decompress, it's time to get on with your life. We'll talk about how to create a retirement lifestyle that's well-suited to you in the section titled, "Curate Your Retirement."

Chapter 6

8 Surprising Ways that Retirement Can Stress You Out

"I wanted a perfect ending. Now I've learned, the hard way, that some poems don't rhyme, and some stories don't have a clear beginning, middle, and end. Life is about not knowing, having to change, taking the moment and making the best of it, without knowing what's going to happen next. Delicious ambiguity."
\- Gilda Radner

When you think about what your retirement lifestyle will be like, what comes to mind? What adjectives would you use to describe what you hope your life will be like?

One that's probably high on your list is "stress-free." You want your retirement years to be more relaxing and less stressful, since you will no longer have to deal with work, your kids will be grown, and you can spend your time doing what you want to do.

In the long run it should work out that way. However, the transition into retirement might be one of the most stressful times of your life. This probably seems counter-intuitive. Shouldn't your graduation from work to leisure be liberating and exciting?

The period of time when you end your working career and enter retirement may be the time when you experience more changes happening simultaneously than at any other time during your life. That's a recipe for high stress.

What causes stress?

The pressure of deadlines at work, competing priorities at work or at home, financial issues, relationship problems, and fear of almost anything are typical situations that can cause stress.

But any life change or any change to your surroundings and your routine can also cause stress. Even positive and welcome changes, such as going off to college, starting a new job, getting married, or moving into a new house, can cause stress.

What will be changing?

Let's take a look at all the things that will be changing in your life simultaneously.

1. Your daily schedule

You may relish the thought of not being rudely awakened by your alarm clock. You may look forward to easing into each day with a leisurely cup of coffee and breakfast. You will certainly not miss your commute.

But this new freedom brings a loss of structure. You may find that you miss not having meetings to attend at designated times throughout the day. You may find that you get less done without having deadlines to meet.

You may actually miss the predictability and the structure you have been accustomed to living with for most of your life.

Some days, you may find that it's already dinner time and you have no idea where the day went. While that may seem appealing at first, before long this will bother you.

2. The people in your daily life

You'll probably see fewer faces during the day. Even though many of the people with whom you come into contact each day may be strangers or casual acquaintances, there is pleasure in human contact and interaction.

Your relationships with the co-workers whom you regard as your friends will change significantly. Despite everyone's sincere wishes to keep in touch, work-based friendships usually fall away quickly. You will no longer have the common bond of the shared work experience. Your familiar channels of communication, whether in person or via company email and instant messaging, will no longer be available.

You will find that social interaction doesn't happen as easily anymore. It now requires more intentional effort to maintain your network of friends and spend time with them.

3. Your job title

Depending on how career-focused you are, your title may mean a lot to you. If your title contains words such as "senior," "chief," or "vice-president," that title carries a certain amount of prestige, status, and empowerment.

Regardless of whether your title is fancy or not, your job title embodies your professional identity. When someone you meet asks what you do and you reply with something like "architect," "teacher," "librarian," "dentist," or "air conditioning technician," your title reflects the knowledge and skill you have and the value you offer to the world.

When you retire, you lose this identity, at least in the present tense. You'll always be a "former" or "retired" something, but that probably won't provide the same level of fulfillment or validation.

You may miss your job title, if that defines a significant part of who you are. You may be surprised to find that you miss your job!

4. Your physical surroundings

Unless you already work from home, your physical surroundings will change. While your cubicle, workstation or company vehicle may not have been luxurious or even comfortable, at least it was the place where you delivered the knowledge and service that provided your income and your sense of purpose. Regardless of whether you enjoy your workplace or despise it, it's what you are accustomed to. Your workplace is your "home away from home," for better or worse.

While you may have a beautiful and comfortable home, spending your entire day there, day in and day out, may bring isolation and cabin fever.

5. Your relationship with your spouse

If you're married or partnered, your relationship with your spouse will change. If your spouse is also home all day, you will now be around him or her almost all the time. No matter how much you love your spouse, suddenly finding yourself in constant contact with him or her may bring stress.

You may need to talk candidly about how much time you wish to spend together and how much time you want to have for individual pursuits. You may also need to renegotiate your daily routines and your division of household duties.

If you retire and your spouse continues to work, you'll have a different challenge. You'll be alone for large amounts of time. The same is true for single people. Rather than being surrounded by co-workers, you'll now be home alone.

We will explore this topic in greater depth in the section titled, "Your Marriage."

6. Your relationship with money

Even if you have saved adequately for retirement or you have a pension that will pay an amount that you can comfortably live on, your relationship with money will change. You'll need less money for things like commuting, work apparel, and perhaps eating out for lunch. However, with more time on your hands, you may find yourself spending more on activities, hobbies, and classes. You may go out shopping when you don't really need anything as an excuse for something to do.

In most cases, you will have to adjust to spending less than you have been accustomed to. While you had a steady work income you may have allowed yourself a certain amount of frivolous, carefree spending. After retirement, you will probably find yourself evaluating each expenditure a little more closely.

It may be unsettling to no longer see those automatic paycheck deposits appearing in your bank account.

*****

If you relocate at the same time you retire or soon thereafter, you will introduce even more disruptive changes into your life.

1. Your friends

Your relationships with friends will change. While today's communication technologies allow people to stay in touch more than ever, there's still nothing like in-person contact.

When you first arrive at your new destination, you will have no local friends. You'll need to prioritize finding new social groups to join in order to start making friends in your new location.

2. Familiar places

The places you are accustomed to visiting will change. You'll need to seek out and discover new stores, restaurants, theaters, doctors, repair companies, and so on.

If you have moved at any time during your life, you have experienced these changes and you know that you can deal with them. But dealing with environmental changes at the same time you deal with all of the issues mentioned above may compound the level of stress in your life.

The more things change at once, the greater the cumulative impact of the changes will be. The whole is greater than the sum of its parts. You can easily deal with one or two changes at a time, but when a lot of things change at once the impact can be overwhelming.

*****

What can you do to minimize and alleviate all of this stress that retirement may bring?

You may be tempted to avoid this stress altogether and just keep working! But fear not! With a few simple strategies, you can take all of these changes in stride and pave the way for a much smoother transition into your fabulous retirement.

1. Start by acknowledging and identifying everything that is changing.

When you can clearly identify and define a problem, you are halfway to solving it. Many people stress out when they retire simply because they don't realize how disruptive the transition from work to leisure can be. They are blindsided by all the changes.

2. Look for ways to spread the changes out over time.

If you're planning to move when you retire, you will probably find it easier to delay the move for six months to a year.

If you are expecting your money situation to change, try living on your retirement budget for a year before you stop working. It's a good reality check for whether you have accurately estimated your living costs for your desired standard of living.

If you are planning to start a new business after you retire, see how much you can plan and get started on while you're still working. You'll hit the ground running. And since your new endeavor will already be a part of your life, it will be something that remains constant rather than another thing that will change.

3. Give yourself some breathing room.

You may have a long list of new activities and pursuits you want to add to your life as soon as you retire. Perhaps you want to play more golf, join a bowling league, start volunteering with an organization, take a long vacation, remodel your house, start writing a book, and more. You may be eager to get started on all these things that you're been looking forward to.

You may think that filling your schedule full of activities will prevent you from becoming bored, but instead you'll be adding to the amount of change that is taking place in your life. Taking on too many new things at once will add stress, not alleviate it. So, spread the new activities out. Things will come along to fill your days soon enough. You'll know when it's time to start adding new things into your life.

You could easily have twenty or thirty years of retirement ahead of you. You don't need to do everything in the first year.

Speaking of taking a long vacation, it's not a good idea to do that immediately upon retiring. You might be dreaming of celebrating the end of your working career by hitting the road in your RV to explore the country, or taking a lengthy cruise or a two-month trip through Europe. But you'll find that there is a lot of paperwork to tend to in the weeks following your last day of work. Your health insurance coverage may change, there will be paperwork related to starting to draw money from your investments and/or pension, and there will be other loose ends to tie up. Being gone for a week won't present a problem, but a lengthier absence probably will.

4. Talk!

If you are married or partnered, talk to your spouse about your concerns. Talk about how your daily lives will change. Share your preferences and desires for when you'll get up, how often you'll eat out, how you'll divide household tasks, and how much time you'll spend together. Your spouse may have his or her own ideas about how you can spend all of your new-found free time – ideas that may involve tackling that long list of to-do items that has developed over many years.

If you have friends who have already retired, talk to them about what their transition was like. Ask them how their actual retirement compares to the preconceived notions they had before they stopped working.

If you are counting on other people to be more available to you after you retire, talk to them too. If you have kids, talk about how much they will want you to visit. Don't assume that your working friends will be available to get together with you more often now that you have more time available to you. They still have to work.

Fortunately, if you can see these challenges coming and take steps to prepare for them, you can head off many of these stressors and start enjoying your fabulous retirement sooner. If you can postpone some changes, such as moving to a new house after you retire, that will give you fewer changes to adapt to at once.

Chapter 7

7 Unexpected Emotions You May Experience After You Retire

"Life is a series of natural and spontaneous changes. Don't resist them; that only creates sorrow. Let reality be reality. Let things flow naturally forward in whatever way they like."
- Lao Tzu

Most people approach retirement with one of two outlooks: eager anticipation or dread. If you have looked forward to retirement for a long time and you envision your retirement as a carefree time of freedom and relaxation, you might expect to feel a great sense of accomplishment and joy for having reached this milestone. If you have anticipated that your retirement will be a time of uncertainty, decline, and boredom, you may enter retirement feeling fearful and depressed.

In either case, after you retire you may experience some emotions that will be totally unexpected and that you might not be prepared for.

Since so many aspects of your life will change when you retire, it's not surprising that you will experience some emotional upheaval. Which emotions you experience, in what order, and at what point after you retire will be unique to you.

Remember that experiencing any of these emotions will probably be a temporary phase, and you'll pass through it. It's helpful to be aware of the possibility that you may feel these things, so that if they hit you it will be less of a shock and you'll be better prepared to deal with them.

Let's take a look at some of the emotions you might experience from time to time during the weeks and months following your retirement.

1. Loss of career identity / lack of purpose

During your working years, you may not realize the extent to which you identify with your job title. Your career identity gives you a sense of purpose and belonging. It represents the value you contribute to the world and the means by which you support yourself and your loved ones.

When you meet someone new and they ask what you do, you have an answer ready to give them.

Of course, you are more than your job title. You may be a spouse, a parent, a brother or sister, a friend, a confidant, a volunteer, a mentor, a role model, and much more. You probably don't realize the extent to which you are various things to other people as well as to yourself.

Most of all, you are a human being - a thinking, breathing, feeling, loving, vital human being.

Viewed in the context of your multi-faceted greater self, you can see that your job title is just a portion of who you really are.

One of the greatest aspects of retirement is that you can create and develop new facets of your identity to replace your job title.

It also helps to realize that most things in life are temporary to one extent or another. You were a child once, but you are no more. Perhaps you were a college student once, but you are no more. Your job title, and the professional identity it represents, is also a hat you wear for a long period of time. But when you retire, you will wear it no more.

Life goes on.
We'll work on creating a new identity in the next chapter.

2. Uncertainty about whether you made the right choice

As with many major decisions in life, you may second-guess yourself after you retire. Some days, you may wonder if you should have kept working longer, perhaps to save more money or because your life feels adrift at that moment.

During the time leading up to your decision to retire, you tried your best to make the right decision. Now that the decision has been made, focus on making the decision right.

You can always make a case for delaying retirement one more year. You'll earn more money. You can delay filing for social security. You'll have health benefits for another year. And with each passing year, your life gets a little shorter. So does the number of years you will have to enjoy your retirement.

At some point, you need to be satisfied that you have enough. In Bronnie Ware's book *The Top Five Regrets of the Dying*, she states that one of the greatest regrets most people have at the end of their lives is that they worked too much and didn't retire sooner.

3. Guilt over no longer working

For your entire adult life up to this point, you have lived with the value that you should work to earn your income. You should pull your own weight. You should be productive and make a meaningful contribution to society.

Retirement disrupts that work ethic. Now, it seems as though money is coming in even though you are no longer working. That's true, but it's not like you have suddenly become a burden on others. The money you are now harvesting from your investments is money that you earned throughout your career and dutifully saved for this day. You have already worked for this money.

Your social security checks are also something you have worked for. Throughout your working years, you gave up some of your income in the form of your social security payroll deduction.

You might also feel guilty for being retired if your spouse and your friends are still working. You might feel reluctant to share how you spent your day engaged in leisure pursuits while everyone else is still working.

We are each on a different path. There are many factors to consider. You might be a little older. Perhaps you saved more or invested better. Maybe you are able to live on less money than they are. Or perhaps they could retire but are choosing to continue working for whatever reasons.

In any case, you would probably never deny your family or friends pleasure over their good fortune, so why should they deny you pleasure over yours?

There's no reason to feel guilty about retiring. You've earned it.

4. Disappointment

If you placed high expectations on what your retirement would be like, you may feel underwhelmed once you experience the reality of day-to-day retirement.

You may be disappointed to discover that retirement is not a permanent vacation. It's easy to imagine that every day will be filled with fun and recreation. If you love playing golf, you may envision that you will play golf every day. Your idealized view of retirement may be moving to a house by the ocean and spending every day on the beach.

While every day in retirement is not fanciful bliss, you will have plenty of time to do the things you enjoy. Some of your days will be consumed by more mundane tasks like grocery shopping, cleaning the house, and paying bills, just like they were during your working years. You will have good days and bad days, just like you have had throughout the rest of your life.

You may experience an "adrenalin rush" when you first retire. At first, the novelty of not having to answer to an alarm clock and being free from your boss and all of your work responsibilities will feel really good. But after the initial rush subsides and you settle into your new day-to-day routine, you may find yourself wondering, "is that all there is?"

Of course that's not all there is. But what comes next is completely up to you. You now have a tremendous opportunity to reinvent yourself and your life. It's up to you to determine what that will look like and get started.

5. Disorientation

Most of your life up to this point has been a predictable routine.

The alarm goes off, you grope for the snooze button two or three times, you finally get up and rush off to work. After work, you come home, check your mail, eat dinner, watch some TV, then head to bed.

You had routines for your days off, too. Every so often you got to take a week or two off, so you either went somewhere or stayed home and knocked some items off your to-do list.

Your particular experience may be a bit different from this, but the point is that you have followed a general script for the past forty or so years.

Regardless of whether you enjoyed or despised your routine, it was consistent. You didn't have to think too much about it. You probably found comfort in the normalcy of your day-to-day life.

Suddenly, that routine is disrupted. No more work, no more vacation weeks. Your life is no longer scripted out for you.

It's easy to feel disoriented. You might feel like a boat that's adrift on the sea, rising and falling on the gentle waves but seemingly heading nowhere.

This feeling should gradually pass as you develop a new routine. Your challenge is to create a new life that contains enjoyable and worthwhile activities and people. You can create a satisfying new life, or you can sit back passively and allow a new life to be created for you by default.

6. Fear and worry

There will be times when you are going to feel fearful about your future.

You're going to worry about whether your money will last.

You're going to wonder whether you or your spouse (or both of you) will suffer illness, injury, or death too soon, robbing you of the opportunity to enjoy years of happy retirement and fulfill those dreams you've held for years.

Whenever the stock market takes a dive or the political climate changes, you will worry about whether your finances will be wiped out and you'll have to live out your remaining days in poverty.

Fear and worry are destructive emotions that never result in a positive outcome and sap you of your happiness.

Most of the things you worry about never come to pass, or at least they never turn out to be as bad as you worried they would be. The few things that do come to pass are going to happen whether you worry about them or not.

In the meantime, you'll be spending the days of your retirement sad and afraid.

Fear is just as bad, if not worse. People will take advantage of you and do bad things to you by playing upon your fears. That's how morally bankrupt politicians convince people to vote for them, or at least to vote against their opponent. That's how unscrupulous people get you to buy things you don't really need, like those 100-day survival packs that you keep under your bed for when the zombie apocalypse comes.

Fear is what leads you to sell all your remaining stock right after a crash, when prices are at their lowest, thereby turning your temporary paper loss into a permanent reality.

I am not saying you should go through life like a naive Pollyanna, blissfully paying no attention to anything happening around you and pretending that life is all rainbows, unicorns, and chocolate-covered cherries. Life brings problems and challenges for you to solve.

You just need to keep your eyes open and your wits about you and deal with these things rationally. Do your best to remain attuned to whether you are making decisions fueled by fear and anxiety or based upon objective information.

Besides, neither you nor I really know what the future holds. Maybe you or your spouse will die next year. Maybe you will be swamped with medical bills. Maybe the terrorists will win. If any of these things happen, they will happen whether you worry about them or not.

That's all the more reason to enjoy today. Don't spoil it with needless worry.

7. Loneliness

According to some studies, nearly half of all retirees report feeling lonely on a regular basis. Some reasons for this are obvious. You're no longer surrounded by people at work. Your spouse may pass away. If you choose to move after you retire, you'll land in a strange city where you don't know anyone.

While it's understandable that you could feel lonely in any of these situations, the solution is largely within your control. You simply need to take the initiative to get out and meet some new people.

Modern technology, including video calling tools such as Skype and Facetime, social media such as Facebook, and even old-fashioned email, makes it easier than ever to stay in touch with people. Granted, electronic communication will never replace face-to-face interaction, but it's a lot better than nothing. Plus, the internet can be very useful for finding local events and groups to join where you can meet people with similar interests.

I'll provide more options in the chapter, "Preventing Loneliness."

PART THREE

Curate Your Retirement

Chapter 8

Create a New Identity

"People often say that this or that person has not yet found himself. But the self is not something one finds, it is something one creates."
- Thomas Szasz

After devoting many years to your career, you have probably come to identify yourself closely with what you do for a living. When you meet someone new and they ask what you do, it's easy to say, "I'm a teacher" or "I'm an engineer" or "I'm a manager," whatever the case may be.

Sometimes after people retire, they suffer from a loss of identity. It probably won't be as satisfying to say, "I'm a retired _____" or simply "I'm retired."

For some people, the word "retired" carries baggage. To some, "retirement" screams "has-been." Some people visualize retirement as those sad last few years of life, when your health deteriorates, you have little money, nothing to do, no reason to live, and you ultimately move into an assisted living facility or nursing home and die. Most of the people you see are doctors and caregivers, and your primary mode of transportation is a motorized wheelchair.

Of course, it doesn't have to be that way at all.

One of the greatest aspects of retiring is the opportunity to rediscover and redefine yourself. With a positive attitude, you can view your post-working years not so much a retirement as a renaissance.

As you probably know, the word "renaissance" was originally coined to describe the time of the great revival of art, literature, and learning in Europe beginning in the 14th century and extending to the 17th century, marking the transition from medieval times to the modern world. The modern meaning is a renewal of life, rebirth, or revival. That sums up what retirement should be all about.

Think back to when you were young. Did you have a vision for what you wanted to do for a career, but you dismissed it because you figured you couldn't make a decent living at it? For example, perhaps you wanted to be an author, painter, golfer, yoga teacher, or jazz musician.

What activities did you give up because the demands of a career and family took over your time? These might include hiking, traveling, reading, playing music, going to the gym, or playing tennis.

The good news is that your retirement years offer you the opportunity to do almost all of these things.

You can choose to pursue avocations you are truly passionate about, without regard to whether or not they will produce income. The amazing thing is, you may be able make some money doing it – maybe a lot!

You could write that epic book, create beautiful music or art, or perform works of service that truly touch people's lives.

You may make the greatest contribution to the world and do the things you become best known for in retirement, not in your working career!

That's pretty mind-blowing when you think about it.

You'll have the time to do many of those things you don't seem to have time for today because of that inconvenient thing called a job. Many active retirees' lives are as full as their lives during their working years – but it's completely different because their schedules are full of the things they really want to do.

In any case, your identity and the pursuits you focus on will change, and so will your spouse's. Hopefully, you'll become new, rejuvenated people. It's a good idea to discuss with your spouse how these changes will impact who you are, your lives together, and how you will view yourselves and each other as you both change.

Give some thought to your new identity. You can name it and define it however you want. You may even have several new identities, depending upon your various interests. Don't worry, nobody is going to accuse you of schizophrenia. And you no longer need to have your job title approved by HR.

Chapter 9

What is Your Retirement Personality Type?

"I am the only person in the world I should like to know thoroughly."
- Oscar Wilde

Retirement is not one-size-fits-all. There are many ways to envision how you'll spend your retirement years.

Identifying your retirement personality type can help you gain clarity about what you want your retirement to be like on a day-to-day basis. You might see yourself in more than one of these categories, and the categories you fit into may change as your retirement progresses.

If you are coupled, it's important to compare your retirement personality type with that of your partner in order to ensure that you both have compatible visions for how you want to enjoy your retirement. If your personality types differ significantly, you will need to make some adjustments and compromises.

Your retirement personality type will influence many of the factors that go into planning your retirement, such as how much money you'll need and where you'll live.

Here are eight different retirement personality types. You'll probably see yourself in at least one and perhaps several.

1. The Perpetual Worker

If you are a Perpetual Worker, some form of work for pay will remain a part of your life for most of your remaining years.

This may take the form of employment, contract work, consulting or entrepreneurial endeavors. It may be full-time, part-time or seasonal. Your line of work may be a continuation of your work career or a job in a different field. But you will continue to be engaged in some pursuit that earns money.

You may remain in the workforce because you need the money, but you could be motivated by other forces as well. You may crave the structure, the challenge or the sense of accomplishment that work brings. Perhaps you view work as a way to maintain social contact with others or a reason to get up and leave home every day. You may need the health benefits that employment provides. If you have worked in a managerial or leadership role you may not be ready to give up the satisfaction of having organizational responsibilities or being in charge.

As a Perpetual Worker, you probably derive your sense of purpose and identity from your job. Once you finally do stop working, be aware that you run the risk of feeling unsettled or adrift because your life has always been centered around your work.

2. The Volunteer

If you are a Volunteer, you share some characteristics with the Perpetual Worker, such as the need to feel productive, the desire for human contact, and wanting a sense of purpose or accomplishment. But you aren't motivated by money – you are driven by a desire to contribute and give back to society.

Volunteering can take many forms. You may volunteer in a social service agency to help people who are less fortunate. You can volunteer as an usher at a concert hall or a docent at a museum. You can share your expertise with students by volunteering as a tutor or mentor. You could travel to serve as a volunteer at a state or national park.

Fortunately, there are bound to be volunteer opportunities no matter where you choose to live.

3. The Doting Grandparent

As a Doting Grandparent, enjoying your family is your greatest priority for your retirement years.

You will probably choose to live as close to your family as possible so that you can share holidays and you won't miss out on your grandchildren's performances, sporting events, and birthday parties. You are happy to be a babysitter and might organize and sponsor family vacations if you are financially able.

The potential downside to being a Doting Grandparent is that your kids may move to follow career opportunities. If this happens, you will be faced with the decision of whether to move to a place that may be a less desirable retirement destination or stay put and have less frequent contact with your kids and grandkids.

4. The Traveler

If you are a Traveler, retirement is the time to hit the road, the skies, and the sea and explore the world.

You might purchase a recreational vehicle and spend months traversing the country. Perhaps you'll rent a home or apartment in a foreign country so that you can explore an area more thoroughly and experience what everyday life is like for the locals. If you can afford it, you may choose to take extended cruises in various parts of the world.

If you are truly committed to traveling, your recreational vehicle might be your home.

5. The Fun Seeker

If you view retirement as a permanent vacation and you look forward to filling each carefree day with recreational activities and entertainment, you are a Fun Seeker.

Your attitude is that because you have worked hard all of your life, now it's time to have fun. You dream of playing golf or tennis every day, joining activity clubs and participating in lots of social events.

While you can participate in a lot of fun activities after you retire, you will probably discover that this vision is a bit idealized. There will still be mundane elements in your daily life such as housecleaning, grocery shopping and doctor appointments. A lifestyle of nothing but play would get old sooner or later.

As a Fun Seeker, your best living option might be a seniors-only active retirement community with a golf course, pickle ball courts, a pool and a club house with dozens of organized activities and clubs to choose from. Since all of your neighbors will also be retired, it will be easier to find activity partners.

6. The Self-Actualizer

If you spent your career doing what would bring in a good paycheck rather than what you are truly passionate about, then you are probably looking forward to retirement as the time when you can finally do what you want to do and become the person that you were meant to be. Perhaps you yearn to express yourself creatively as an artist, writer, photographer, musician or, craftsperson. If this describes you, you're a Self-Actualizer.

You may already have a well-formed vision for how you will live your life as your true self. If not, your retirement may be a time to embark on a journey to discover your passion.

You can explore a variety of new things until you find what makes your heart sing. For you, retirement is a time for reinventing yourself and seeking fulfillment.

If you are a Self-Actualizer, you will probably want to live in a thriving city with a plethora of community resources such as performance venues, museums, colleges, bohemian neighborhoods, and seemingly endless opportunities for things to do.

7. The Lifelong Learner

If it's important to you to stay mentally sharp and engaged with the world, you are a Lifelong Learner.

Your retirement lifestyle will include taking classes on whatever interests you at a local community center, college, or lifelong learning center. You'll make good use of your local library. You'll want to live in a place that has plenty of educational resources.

For your vacations, you may look to Road Scholar (formerly Elderhostel) for trips that have an educational focus. You will probably prefer destinations with historical importance or that afford you the opportunity to discover new places and cultures.

8. The Decelerator

If you view retirement as a time to just kick back and relax, you're a Decelerator.

Like the Fun Seeker, you believe that you have worked hard for your entire career and now you deserve a life that's free of stress and responsibility. Unlike the Fun Seeker, you have no particular activities or pursuits in mind.

You hope to live without an alarm clock or a schedule and simply let each day unfold as it will. Doing nothing is fine. You hope to disengage from political news and world problems and have as little to worry about as possible.

You may envision retiring to some beautiful, quiet, idyllic place like a beach, a tropical island, or a cabin by a lake or in the mountains where your environment will be relaxed and serene.

While this sounds wonderful, sooner or later you will probably get bored. You risk becoming a couch potato and getting insufficient exercise. You may discover that you need more human contact and mental stimulation, and you want to live a more purposeful life.

What's your retirement type?

Chapter 10

Design Your Day

"How we spend our days is, of course, how we spend our lives."
- Annie Dillard

Now is the time to be intentional and design how you want your days – and your life – to be.

Aside from occasional weekend or vacation days, your retirement may be the first time in your life when you have been fully in control of how you spend your days on an on-going basis.

During your working career, your work schedule was determined for you. Even if you had a flexible work schedule or you were an entrepreneur, you had meetings, deadlines, and long lists of things to accomplish that drove how you spent your time.

Before that, while you were in school, your life was driven by your school schedule. Your hours outside of class were consumed by your homework and project assignments.

During your summer breaks and as a pre-school child you had more latitude with how you spent your time. But even then, you were constrained by what you were allowed to do and your free time still occurred within time frames that were controlled by your parents.

Now, you have total control. Your daily schedule and your calendar are a blank slate. You are literally standing on the verge of the next great chapter in your life. Now you have a prime opportunity to be intentional and design your days - and your life - to be the way you want them to be.

Just as the curator at an art museum selects which pieces of art will be displayed in the museum, you can think of yourself as the curator for your life. You can select which pieces will be included in your life at any given time. And like the artwork at a museum, you can rotate things in and out of your life as time moves on.

How will this next phase of your life unfold?

Over the next few days and weeks, find some times when you can sit in a quiet place with no interruptions or distractions. Think about the following questions and write down your thoughts.

- What do you want to add to your life?
- What do you want to remove from your life (besides your job)?
- What do you want to include in your daily routine? For example: meditating, exercising, reading, a creative pursuit (writing, painting, practicing an instrument), walking your dog, or sipping coffee or tea while reading the news.
- What do you want to do at various times during the week? For example: going to the gym three times a week, group meetings, rehearsals, game night, date night, or going to church.
- What do you want to accomplish within the next year? For example: household projects, travel (where?), taking a class, or starting a new hobby or activity.

Now, develop a plan for what a typical day and a typical week will look like. Don't forget to leave time for the mundane things like preparing meals, house cleaning, laundry, and grocery shopping. Sadly, there's no retiring from them!

How tightly you schedule your days is up to you. If you thrive on routine and structure, you might want to schedule each day of the week down to the hour or half-hour. If you want your retirement to be a little less structured, you can simply develop a list of what you'll do on a typical Monday, Tuesday, Wednesday, and so on. You may choose to break the day down into broad categories like morning, afternoon, and evening.

A lot will depend on how comfortable or antsy you feel with a lot of time on your hands.

Of course, you will probably deviate from your schedule more often than not. A friend may call and invite you to lunch. If it's a beautiful day, you might decide to go have fun outside. One of the greatest joys of retirement is that you have the flexibility to ditch your plan and go with the flow!

Your life will continue to evolve and your daily routine will adapt. But going through this exercise will help you articulate what is important to you and what you want your life to look like.

It will give you direction and keep you active and engaged.

It will prevent you from sinking into a boring, purposeless rut of wasting your days in front of the TV or the computer.

It will encourage you to form new lifestyle habits that will serve you well during the coming years.

If you don't fill your life intentionally with the activities that truly bring value to you, then trivial and unrewarding things will easily rush in to take up the space. There's always something around the house that needs fixing or cleaning. People will ask you to volunteer for this or that. There's an infinite amount of brain candy on the internet.

The sad truth is that when many people quit working, whatever else was already part of their lives simply expands to take the place of work. Most people don't change their habits and their lifestyle much after they retire.

You can choose to design a happy, fulfilling retirement, or simply stand by and let retirement happen to you.

If you have great things in mind for how you're going to spend your retirement years, you will need to mindfully create the habits, routines, and priorities to make them happen.

Chapter 11

To Enjoy the Retirement of Your Dreams, What Are You Willing to Change?

"When people are ready to, they change. They never do it before then, and sometimes they die before they get around to it. You can't make them change if they don't want to, just like when they do want to, you can't stop them."
- Andy Warhol

It's easy to imagine an ideal retirement lifestyle, filled with stress-free days in which you are engaging in all those self-fulfilling pursuits you've always dreamed of but never had time for. You probably have a nice list of things you would like to do and places you want to go after you retire. Maybe you have an actual bucket list.

But how many of those things on your list will you actually do? Chances are, not very many.

Why?

Because many of those items on your list require you to do something differently than you have been accustomed to for most of your life. They may require you to change your habits or change the way you live. Some of them require a lot of planning. Some require you to leave your comfort zone.

The truth is, you are a creature of habit. A lot of those habits have been engrained in you for most of your life.

What will it take to get you started on the path towards the ideal retirement you envision?

Simply put, it takes change. By changing nothing, nothing changes.

It's one thing to imagine your ideal retirement lifestyle. It's quite another matter to change your day-to-day life and your lifelong habits to enable that lifestyle to happen.

What new things are parts of your ideal retirement lifestyle?

If you want to take art classes or music lessons or learn a new language, when are you going to start?

If you dream of moving to another place or even another country, many aspects of your day-to-day life will change. You'll have to learn a new place, which may be very different. You'll have to find new favorite places to shop, find new doctors and other service providers, and make new friends. How do you feel about making those changes?

If you are accustomed to eating out often or spending money on whatever shiny new things you see in stores, are you willing to change your habits to spend more judiciously?

If you have relied upon your co-workers for much of your socialization, are you willing to change so that you will take more initiative to get out and meet more people?

The sad truth is that when most people quit working, whatever else was part of their lives simply expands to take the place of work, especially television. Most people don't change their habits and their lifestyle much after they retire.

If you have great things in mind for how you're going to spend your retirement years, you will need to mindfully change your habits, routines and priorities to make them happen.

Change is intentional.

As the old cliché goes, the definition of "insanity" is doing the same things and expecting a different result.

What do you need to change in order to achieve your ideal retirement?

Chapter 12

To Enjoy the Retirement of Your Dreams, What are You Willing to Let Go Of?

"One part of wisdom is knowing what you don't need any more and letting it go."
- Jane Fonda

After you retire, a world of possibilities opens up for what you can do with your life.

You can spend more time doing things you're passionate about, such as writing, playing music, creating art, or volunteering.

You can travel more, without being limited to a finite number of vacation days each year.

You can spend more time on physical activities, such as hiking, biking, or playing golf.

You can allow more time for enjoying hobbies, taking courses, reading, or enjoying cultural events.

The possibilities seem endless! After adding many of these things to your life, you could easily find yourself busier than you were during your working years. But filling your life with busyness probably won't make you happier. In fact, it could leave you more stressed out.

As it turns out, your happiness in retirement could be determined as much by what you remove from your life as what you add. Finding ways to eliminate the noise and the needless complications should make for a much more satisfying life.

Here are four things you could eliminate from your life to be happier in retirement.

1. Activities you don't enjoy

Once you are retired, you will have more time for chores such as cleaning your house and maintaining your yard. If you truly enjoy gardening and landscaping, that's great. That may even be among the things you are looking forward to having more time for.

But if your vision of a satisfying retirement doesn't include a lot of time spent on home and yard upkeep, look into ways to reduce or eliminate it. Consider removing high-maintenance trees and plants from your yard or replacing your grass with artificial turf. Moving to an apartment, condo or retirement community will eliminate your yard maintenance altogether. Moving to a smaller home will reduce the amount you have to clean indoors, or you could hire a cleaning service if your financial situation will support that.

2. Obligations that don't bring fulfillment

After you retire, people might easily assume that you have a lot of free time on your hands. In their eyes, you are now a prime candidate for serving on committees and boards. This can be enjoyable and fulfilling, but only say yes if you really want to do it. You shouldn't feel obligated to accept a commitment just because you have the available time or the required skills.

Similarly, if you live near your children and grandchildren, your children might assume that you are readily available on call to babysit the grandchildren. Of course you love your grandkids and want to spend time with them, but it's up to you to decide how much time you are willing to devote to looking after them and say no when that time is exceeded.

3. Possessions you no longer use

Getting rid of items in your house that you haven't used for years is both therapeutic and practical. Rooms that are neat and uncluttered are more inviting and pleasant than rooms full of things crammed into every available space. You will have less to clean and keep track of.

Chances are, you waste time looking for things you know you own but can't find. Worse, you may end up buying duplicates of the things you can't find or have forgotten that you own.

If you are currently renting storage space to hold your extra stuff, emptying it will save you the monthly rental fee as well as the time you spend driving there and rooting through boxes to find what you're looking for. Most items you are keeping in a storage facility are things you really have no further need for, but you can't bring yourself to throw away. When you finally do dispose of them, it will be a weight off your shoulders.

Try to take a fresh look at everything in your life and ask yourself whether it's really necessary and whether it can be eliminated or made simpler.

4. People you don't enjoy

Life is too precious and too short to spend with people who are negative and who drain your energy. Some personal development experts claim that you are the average of the five people you associate with the most, so surround yourself with people who are positive, supportive, and fun.

Of course, you should be available to help your friends through difficult times, such as a death in the family or recuperating from an injury. But if you have people in your life who are constant whiners or complainers, disengage from them. If you know people who are petty gossipers, distance yourself and don't get caught up in their drama. If you have friends who only call or visit you when they want to talk about themselves or need a shoulder to cry on but who show little concern for you, replace them with friends who are more caring and uplifting.

*****

Humans are creatures of habit. By the time you retire, your lifestyle habits have been engrained for many years. Many people and many of the activities you have been engaged in probably came into your life by happenstance or for reasons that are no longer relevant. Do they still provide value?

Retirement offers you an opportunity to redesign your life into one that is more happy and fulfilling. Try to look at everything you do, everything you own and everyone who is part of your life with fresh eyes. Ask yourself whether each activity, thing, or person is contributing to the retirement you want, and if not, make a change.

You have worked hard all your life, now it's time to live life on your terms.

Designing your ideal retirement lifestyle is as much about what you remove from your life as what you add to it.

What activities or obligations can you let go if, in order to make your life happier and have more time and/or money to devote to what you really want?

What would make your life simpler, easier, and more fun?

Chapter 13

Why You Still Need Time Management after You Retire

"Growing old is no more than a bad habit which a busy person has no time to form."
- Andre Maurois

You may believe that you no longer need to manage your time after you retire. Perhaps you regard time management as something you get to leave behind when your working career ends. After all, you have been a slave to your work schedule for decades.

If you are not retired yet, you may envision that the ultimate retirement lifestyle will consist of getting up whenever you want, eating whenever you want, doing whatever you want or nothing at all, and going to bed whenever you want.

That may be therapeutic for the first few weeks after you leave your job. It can help you decompress from decades of work. But that approach won't remain satisfying for very long.

With no discipline or direction, you'll discover that days and weeks will pass without doing much that's meaningful. The next thing you know, months will have passed and you'll have no idea where the time went or what you did. You will end up bored, unhappy and sedentary. You'll spend most of your time in front of the TV or the computer. That's probably not what you had in mind for your retirement. It's not very healthy, either.

Sooner or later, you'll discover that you still need some form of time management. However, you will probably approach it differently than you did while you were working.

"Quality of life is not affected as much by the amount of free time that a retiree has, but on how effectively the person manages this time on hand," says Wei-Ching Wang of the I-Shou University in Taiwan, who has studied how retirees manage their time and their resulting quality of life.

You will probably find that a happy and satisfying retirement lifestyle consists of a mix of activities that provide physical activity, mental stimulation, socialization with others, and personal fulfillment. Add in the mundane tasks such as cooking, shopping, laundry, and household chores and your life might seem overloaded again. You will need some form of time management system to prioritize these competing interests and find time for it all.

Which system you use is up to you. You can use computer applications such as Outlook or Google Calendar, a phone app, a traditional paper day planner, a white board, or even sticky notes – whatever works for you. Trello.com is good for managing tasks and to-do lists, and so is a simple pad of paper.

If there are things you want to do every day or on a certain number of days per week, such as meditating, writing, or going for a walk, schedule them.

It's fine to alter your schedule or postpone some things until tomorrow. That's part of the freedom of retirement. But if you find yourself postponing things consistently, you should ask yourself whether the items on your schedule are things you really want to do or if they are just things you feel you should do.

Do your best to limit your time on the internet and watching TV. Decide how much time each day you are willing to devote to those passive pursuits, and do your best to stick to it. You may opt to schedule this time. For example, you might allot a half hour to check email and Facebook each morning and a half hour each evening. Perhaps you can use watching TV as a reward for completing everything on your to-do list each day.

It's possible to go to the other extreme, too. You can fill each 15-minute block of time with every little thing you hope to do throughout the day, such as preparing meals, reading, answering emails, paying bills, and so forth. But it's unlikely that you will stick to a schedule that is so regimented that it seems like you're still at work. You probably won't enjoy it, either.

If the idea of maintaining a daily schedule just doesn't appeal to you, you can take a less time-based approach. First thing each morning, write down three things you want to get done that day. You may prefer to make this list before you go to bed the night before. Then, once you have accomplished those three things, you can give yourself permission to spend the rest of the day doing whatever you want.

You will probably end up with a balance of scheduled activities, unscheduled time to spend however you like, and time allotted to your to-do list. The exact mix is up to you.

As a retired person, you will become more conscious of the fact that time is more finite and it seems to pass more quickly. Therefore, it's important to use the time you still have in a way that is satisfying, memorable, and purposeful.

Chapter 14

Preventing Loneliness

"I've learned that every day you should reach out and touch someone. People love a warm hug, or just a friendly pat on the back."
- Maya Angelou

When you retire from work, you retire from pressure, stress, deadlines, performance reviews, boring meetings, and that annoying guy down the aisle who spends all day making personal phone calls that everyone can hear.

But you will also leave behind something that is more important than you may realize: human contact. While most of your colleagues probably aren't close personal friends, just being around people provides a certain level of socialization that you will miss once you retire.

A recent study by the University of California at San Francisco revealed that 43% of the people they surveyed who were over 60 years old reported feeling lonely on a regular basis. Two-thirds of the adults who said they were lonely live with a spouse or other partner, which indicates that you shouldn't rely upon your spouse to be your sole source of companionship.

While you work, social contact happens easily and automatically. After you retire, you can still find plenty of ways to stay socially engaged, but it requires a little more initiative on your part.

Here are seven ways to stay socially active and prevent loneliness after you retire.

1. Take classes

Whether it's an art class, a cooking class, a language class, or a salsa dancing class, you are bound to meet other people with similar interests.

Your local community center or library probably offers inexpensive classes covering a wide variety of topics. Your local college may have programs in which seniors can attend classes that have empty seats for free on a non-credit basis.

2. Join or organize a club

A book discussion group, an investment club, a restaurant-of-the-week club, a wine-tasting club, or other group based around a common interest will bring people together. Some of these groups will provide mental stimulation as well.

Check the activity calendar at your local community center or use an online tool such as Meetup.com to find an existing group or start one of your own.

Toastmasters clubs provide an excellent venue to meet new people and learn their stories, share your knowledge and experience, and become a better speaker.

3. Volunteer

One of the best ways to find a sense of purpose and happiness is to help others who are less fortunate.

Volunteering is also a great way to add more culture into your life and meet people at the same time. You can become a docent or tour guide at a museum or an usher at a concert hall, for example.

If you have business or teaching skills, you can become a mentor. You can join a local service club such as Lions or Kiwanis.

4. Join an activity group – or start one

This could be a hiking group or a group that walks up and down the halls of shopping malls. There are groups that take day trips to local points of interest. A local gym may offer exercise groups for yoga, aerobics, water aerobics, and more that are targeted for seniors.

5. Join a local chorus or band

Most communities have local choruses and bands that welcome people of all ages and ability levels. Don't worry if it's been years since you have sung or played your instrument. You will be surprised at how quickly your skills return.

Pursuing an artistic endeavor is an excellent way to nourish your creativity as well as providing a way to meet others.

6. Call, visit, or write to a friend every day

Today, it is easier than ever to reconnect with friends from all stages of your life using social media tools such as Facebook.

While social media provides a means for initial contact and surface-level interaction, you can cultivate more meaningful connections with people by calling them, writing a personal letter or email or, if they are local, getting together occasionally.

7. Invite people over

You don't have to throw lavish, expensive parties. You can simply invite a few people over for card games or board games, a potluck, or a movie night.

Don't worry if your home is modest or if it's not spotless from floor to ceiling. People are coming to enjoy spending time with you and the other guests, not to inspect your home.

*****

Loneliness doesn't have to be a characteristic of your retirement years. With some possibility thinking and a little bit of effort, you can discover or create a variety of physical activities, mentally stimulating activities, and fulfilling activities that involve meaningful interaction with other people.

PART FOUR

Your Marriage

Chapter 15

8 Conversations Every Couple Needs to Have

"Marriage requires a constant rhythm of adaptation between two people who are changing."
- Mary Catherine Betson

Hopefully, you have at least a general idea of how you want your life to unfold in the years to come. You probably have some ideas, whether vague or specific, about where you would like to live, where you hope to travel, when you hope to retire, and an assortment of dreams and bucket list items you'd like to do someday.

Have you shared these dreams, desires, and goals with your spouse?

How closely do they align with those of your spouse?

Do you know what his or her dreams, desires, and goals are well enough to describe them accurately?

You might be surprised how many couples haven't had these conversations, or how many are operating under incorrect assumptions. It's easy to envision your ideal future, with your spouse by your side, without actually getting your spouse's input and buy-in.

It's easy to assume that your spouse envisions the same future that you do. For every couple, there are many potential sources of difference which require both partners to talk and be flexible in order to find the right balance.

Here are eight conversations you and your spouse will benefit from having - not all in one sitting, of course!

1. When do you plan to retire? Do you plan to retire at all?

Cases in which one spouse retires before the other happen frequently. Perhaps there's an age difference of ten or twenty years. Maybe one spouse is laid off, accepts an early retirement package, or qualifies for his or her employer's retirement benefits sooner that the other one. Or it could be that one spouse is more engaged in a fulfilling career while the other has reached a career dead-end and is ready to move on.

Having one working spouse and one retired spouse is manageable, but it requires some conversation to align on expectations. If the first retired spouse dreams of extensive traveling, that will have to be postponed – unless that spouse wants to travel alone or with others, and that's OK with the working spouse.

Perhaps the working spouse will now expect a home-cooked meal waiting at home each day after a long day at work, and he or she will expect the retired spouse to do a lot more of the housework.

What if one spouse says he or she doesn't want to retire, and wants to work as long as possible?

We will address the challenges of being a mixed-retirement couple in the next chapter.

2. How much money do you need to have saved?

This is a complicated question in any case, and the answer depends a lot on what kind of lifestyle you hope to enjoy after you retire.

Do you wish to live in an upscale retirement community and travel extensively?

Are you willing to downsize and be more frugal in order to retire sooner or make up for not having saved enough?

Do you want to have money left over to leave to your heirs or spend it all on yourselves?

You have probably seen many different guidelines for how much you need to save and what percentage of your working income you will need to live comfortably in retirement. These are all averages. Your needs may vary significantly based on many factors.

Be aware that in spite of your best efforts to budget and plan, you will not be immune to unexpected expenditures such car repairs, house repairs, and medical or dental incidents. Be sure to allow enough of a cushion in your budget to cover these unforeseen expenses when they arise.

Just as money matters are an essential discussion topic during your working years, how much money you'll need for your future is definitely something to talk about.

3. Where and how do you want to live?

First, there's the question of whether you both want to move somewhere else after you retire or stay right where you are. Perhaps you want to stay in the same area, but downsize to a smaller home.

If you're both inclined to move, there's literally a world of possibilities for where you might choose to live.

There's also the question of how you want to live. This ties in closely with the subject of money, as discussed above.

Do you want to live in a senior community or stay in the mainstream?

Do you hope to live lavishly or frugally?

Do you want to travel the continent in a recreational vehicle?

Do you want to move to a foreign country?

To help guide your discussion, it will be helpful to establish what criteria are most important to you. This will provide a framework that will make it easier to focus on places you'll be more likely to enjoy and avoid places that may seem attractive but lack important qualities you desire or need.

4. What activities do you plan to pursue?

This question is largely self-explanatory, but it's important for you and your spouse to compare your ideas for how you will spend your time.

How closely do your ideas align?

And perhaps more important, which of your desired activities are things you can do together as a couple and which will you do on your own?

Your visions of how much time you spend at home vs. outside the home may be quite different.

5. How much time do you plan to spend together, without driving each other crazy?

Of course, you love your spouse. But do you want to be with him or her 24/7?

One of you may envision spending all your time together and doing everything together. The other may envision spending some time alone for reading or participating in projects and activities that don't involve the other person. It's important to align on the ratio of one to the other.

During your working career, work dictates that you spend a lot of time apart, unless you own a business together or you both work from home. After both of you stop working, you will see a lot more of each other.

As much as you love your spouse and enjoy his or her company, being together constantly will change the dynamic between the two of you.

Now more than ever, it's important to talk and share your feelings and concerns with each other.

It may be helpful to establish regular times that you will spend together, such as meals, mid-afternoon breaks, and "date night" evenings.

6. What will your social life look like after you retire?

Along with discussing how much time you wish to spend together and how much time you wish to spend on your individual pursuits, you may also wish to discuss whether all of your friends will be mutual friends that you enjoy together or whether you want to maintain some separate friendships.

This will probably be a continuation of how you maintained friendships during your working years. If one partner's circle of friends consists largely of people from outside of work while the other had primarily work friendships, this will require some adjustment on the part of the person with the work friendships.

In some cases, one partner may be the one who serves as the social coordinator and takes the lead in setting up times to get together with your friends. You need to make sure that both partners are having their social needs met.

7. How will your division of household responsibilities change?

You will probably need to re-negotiate your division of household responsibilities.

Perhaps while you both worked you hired a cleaning service and a landscaping service, but now you will be doing those jobs yourselves.

In cases where one partner worked full-time and the other worked only part-time or was a full-time homemaker, or in cases where one partner traveled extensively for work but no longer does, realigning household chores may be in order.

The retiring worker may feel that his days will now be free for all the golfing, reading, and TV-watching he desires, without considering that the homemaker will have to prepare meals and clean house for the rest of their lives.

8. What family obligations and responsibilities will you have?

Your retirement visions probably focus primarily on you and your spouse. However, other people in your lives may complicate the picture, and the two of you may have differing views on how you will deal with these situations.

Here are just a few examples:

- An adult child asks to live with you, perhaps due to unemployment or a divorce
- You are asked to help care for grandchildren
- One or both of you have aging parents that need additional care, perhaps including moving in with you

Scenarios such as these can impact many aspects of your retirement. In addition to the financial impact, they may also dictate your choice for where to live, how much you can travel, and how much free time you have.

One of you may feel that you've earned your retirement, and you need to stand firm in not letting these requests and situations hijack your golden years. The other may feel a stronger pull to help the family members in need. It's something to talk about.

It's also worth discussing how much time you want to spend visiting family members, and how important it is to each of you to live near them. You may have to make some choices regarding which family members you will live close to.

Chapter 16

How to Address the Challenges of Being a Mixed-Retirement Couple

"A retired husband is often a wife's full-time job."
- Ella Harris

It's not uncommon for two-career couples to retire at different times. This may happen when there is a significant age difference or if one spouse retires sooner than planned due to an unexpected layoff or an irresistible early retirement incentive package. In other cases, one spouse may feel burnt out and ready to throw in the towel while the other spouse is at the peak of his or her career and wants to keep going for a few more years.

Whatever the circumstances, mixed-retirement marriages are situations ripe for resentment and stress. For a time, you and your spouse will have to coexist in different realities, something for which you may be ill-prepared. Here are seven tips that will help you and your spouse adjust to having one spouse work while the other is retired.

1. Go to bed and get up at the same time.

The retired spouse might prefer to be a night owl and may relish the idea of not waking up to an alarm clock. But maintaining separate sleep schedules will lead to a decrease in closeness and quality time for you and your spouse to share. Plus, waking up or preparing for bed while the other spouse is trying to sleep may lead to interrupted sleep and annoyance.

It may be helpful for the retired spouse to get a part-time job that starts at the same time as the working spouse's job, or find a regular volunteer commitment or activity that starts at a similar time.

2. Renegotiate household chores.

The retired spouse can take on extra chores, which he or she can perform while the other spouse is still at work. The working spouse will genuinely appreciate this, and it will allow the couple to spend more time enjoying each other's company during evenings and weekends.

However, if you are the working spouse you should be prepared to accept that the retired spouse may approach some chores differently than you, such as loading the dishwasher or folding the laundry.

Perhaps the greatest potential for marital conflict occurs when the working spouse feels that the retired spouse isn't doing enough around the house. The retired spouse feels that he or she is entitled to a life of leisure after decades of working, while the working spouse still maintains the burden of working and then coming home to a list of chores.

3. Have honest conversations about how the change in income will impact you.

Most people will receive less income from their retirement savings than they enjoyed while they worked. Both you and your spouse should discuss how your spending patterns will change as a result of having less income. This may be particularly relevant for the retired spouse, who will now have more idle hours and may be inclined to spend that time shopping.

4. The retired spouse can focus on projects that don't include the other person.

Chances are, you have a list of projects that you have been hoping to get to someday when you have the time. If you are the spouse that retires first, you have the opportunity to check these items off of your to-do list. Then when your spouse retires, you'll have more time to spend together.

5. The retired spouse should remain engaged with the world.

Once you are both retired, you will be able to spend time doing things together. But until then, the retired spouse should take steps to avoid being isolated at home alone all day.

Some retired spouses find part-time jobs primarily to get out of the house and stay engaged with people.

If you are the retired spouse, limit your time watching TV or using the computer so that you don't form sedentary habits that are unhealthy and may be difficult to break later.

6. Remain aware of the working spouse's needs.

Once you are retired, you may have little interest in hearing about job-related matters, but your working spouse will appreciate being able to talk about what happened at work that day. Be aware that the working spouse may want to relax and decompress after a hard day at work, while the retired spouse may be eager to start doing things together.

7. Be patient while your spouse adjusts to retirement.

Everyone goes through a number of adjustments when they retire, which are discussed throughout this book.

If the retired spouse was accustomed to a highly scheduled day, he or she may find it challenging to adjust to a much less structured routine.

The retired spouse will experience less contact with other people during the day, especially in cases where most of his or her friends were co-workers.

The retired spouse may struggle with a loss of purpose or work identity.

All of these changes may be difficult for the working spouse to comprehend, but it will be helpful for the working spouse to have empathy for the changes the retired spouse is experiencing.

PART FIVE

Retired and Single

Chapter 17

How to Survive and Thrive as a Single Person in Retirement

"People with lifelong friendships and ties to local nonprofessional organizations did not have to fear that isolation would accompany retirement, old age, or losing a spouse. Overburdened householders could count on the assistance not only of their own extended families, but of the American tradition of neighborliness."
- Judith Martin

Much of the information you read about planning for and living during your retirement is heavily focused on couples. Single retirees have a few unique concerns that often aren't comprehended or addressed by websites, books, senior living communities, and other information sources.

Even if you are married now, consider that one of you will experience being single at some point, unless you and your spouse pass away at the same time. Later in this chapter, I will suggest several things you can consider now that will make life easier for the surviving spouse when that time comes.

One of the greatest fears that most people harbor is the fear of dying alone or spending your final years lonely, bored, and confined in a retirement home.

With proper planning, it doesn't have to be this way.

For some people, being single is nothing new.

Generally speaking, single seniors fit into one of two broad categories: those who have been single for much or all of their lives, and those who have been married for most of their adult lives and have recently become single as a result of divorce or the passing of their spouse.

Long-term singles have an advantage in that they are already accustomed to living alone. They are adept at making friends, finding activities and groups to join, and maintaining a support network. They are self-sufficient and comfortable with spending time alone. In fact, many singles relish their independence and autonomy, and they usually aren't looking to find a partner. They are quite happy being single. They have more freedom, can budget and spend as they see fit, travel where and when they want, and participate in the activities that are most rewarding to them.

The biggest challenge that long-term singles face is that they may have saved less for retirement, because they have been solely responsible for maintaining their household on only one paycheck throughout their working years. Women may be at an additional disadvantage due to gender-based pay discrepancies, which leaves less money for retirement savings.

People who become single after being coupled for many years face a significant lifestyle adjustment that could easily last beyond the bereavement period. Their vision for how they would spend their retirement probably centered on how they would spend retirement as a couple. Now, they will need to recalibrate their plans to reflect their new reality of being single in retirement.

On the other hand, the surviving spouse may be better situated financially, assuming that both spouses saved for retirement or, in the case of single-earner households, the breadwinner saved with the anticipation of a retirement for two people. The surviving spouse may also benefit from a life insurance payout.

In this chapter, I'll cover three areas of special concern to single retirees: socialization, support, and living arrangements.

1. Socialization

While you may value having some solitude in your life, you shouldn't spend all your time at home. Make it a point to get out of the house often.

You don't have to have a companion to enjoy a restaurant meal, take a day trip, or go to a movie, concert, or museum. This can be a big adjustment for a newly single person after years of marriage. It's OK to take yourself out on a date every now and then. It's far better to go out and do things that you enjoy on your own than to sit at home alone just because you have no one to go out with.

2. Support

You have probably thrived on taking care of yourself independently, but as you get older it's important to cultivate a support network of trusted people who can drive you to appointments and check in on you occasionally. If you don't have family members in the area who are willing and able to assist you in this capacity, you'll need to rely on friends and neighbors.

Many medical procedures are done on an outpatient basis and hospital stays are short and shrinking, but you will probably need to have someone transport you home and visit regularly to assist you during your convalescence. Home care aides are an option, but that can get expensive.

If you are healthy and active now, you may not require the support of others for many years to come. But it never hurts to have a network in place now. You shouldn't wait until you need help to figure out who can assist you. Besides, it will be awkward to try to develop a friendship with someone when it's obvious that you have an immediate need for them.

The people you select for your support network need to know several important pieces of information, such as who your insurance carrier is, where to find a list of medications you are taking, what you are allergic to, and contact information for other key family members or friends.

If you aren't surrounded by a sufficient support network of friends, family, and neighbors, research whether there are senior support organizations in your area and what services they can provide. If you are planning to move to a new locale in retirement, the existence of such an organization would be a good criterion for you to consider.

3. Living Arrangements

Long-term singles are accustomed to living alone, and may be able to do so long into retirement. But the time will come sooner or later when living with others or living in a close-knit community becomes necessary. Here are a couple options for living arrangements that can provide support and delay the need to move to an assisted living facility.

Co-housing communities are intentional communities of private homes clustered around a shared space. Each attached or single family home has traditional amenities, including a private kitchen. Shared spaces typically feature a common house, which may include a large kitchen and dining area, laundry, and recreational spaces. Neighbors commit to being part of the community for everyone's mutual benefit. They collaboratively plan community activities, manage shared spaces, and share resources such as tools and lawnmowers.

Most co-housing communities are multi-generational, although there are some that are focused on retirees. Multi-generational communities are advantageous in many ways, although some younger neighbors may not fully appreciate the needs of elder residents, and providing care may be more than they have interest or time for.

Shared housing is just what it sounds like – two or more unrelated adults sharing a home. This housing model formed the basis of the classic sitcom "The Golden Girls" and the similar and more recent "Hot in Cleveland."

This may take the form of a homeowner renting one or more bedrooms to someone else, or two or more people sharing a lease on a house or apartment. In either case, it's important to select your roommate(s) carefully and have an agreement in writing, signed by all parties, which specifies the financial arrangements, household responsibilities, ground rules, rules for parties and overnight guests, and any other areas for potential misunderstanding that may arise.

If You Are Married Now

If you are married now, don't count on your spouse to be your sole source of companionship and support.

In many marriages, the spouses have divided up tasks. For example, one may handle all the financial matters, while the other one maintains the contact information for all the friends and relatives. Make sure both of you know enough about what the other one does so that you can take over if the other one becomes incapacitated or dies.

It would be a good idea to write down key information and keep it in a secure place where either spouse can find it if necessary. This includes logins and passwords, instructions, and contact information for your financial advisor, attorney, insurance agents, relatives, etc.

Although you both dream about and plan for a happy retirement spent together, you should devote some thought to how you will live if you survive your spouse.

Chapter 18

The Joys of Traveling Solo

"Do not fear to step into the unknown. For where there is risk, there is also reward. "
- Lori Hard

Traveling solo might be the one of the biggest challenges that single retirees face, especially if you're accustomed to traveling with your spouse. When one half of a couple dies, the surviving spouse may be reluctant to travel alone for anything more adventurous than a visit to family members.

Regardless of whether you've been single for most of your life or you're newly single following a divorce or the death of your spouse, there's no need to give up on your dreams of traveling after you retire.

You might also find yourself traveling solo if you retire before your spouse, your spouse is not interested in traveling, or if he or she is not able to travel.

The hardest step will probably be to convince yourself to go. Once you do, you will discover that traveling solo is one of the most rewarding experiences you can have in your lifetime.

There are many advantages to traveling solo.

When you're on your own, can travel at your own pace, do the things that interest you, eat where and when you like, and splurge where you want to splurge.

You don't have to compromise with a partner when one of you wants to do something the other doesn't or when one of you is ready to leave a museum and the other wants to stay.

You can relax for a day if you're tired or keep going when you feel energetic and engaged.

You will absorb more of your surroundings when you travel alone. When you travel with others, it's natural to direct a lot of your focus toward your partner or group. While it's wonderful to form bonds with others based on shared experiences, you'll miss the full range of sights, sounds and smells that are available all around you.

You're also less likely to interact with local people or fellow travelers, so you'll miss out on the interesting information they may have to share.

Of course, there are disadvantages to traveling solo, too.

When you're on your own, you don't have a built-in dining companion. But that doesn't have to be awkward. You can sit at a sidewalk café and enjoy people-watching.

Traveling by yourself is usually more expensive, because you don't have a partner to share the cost of accommodations or taxis.

Cruise ships are a good option, as are group tours. However, most cruises add a single supplement, which is an additional charge to make up for having only one customer in a room instead of two, which makes them more expensive. A few cruise ships now offer smaller rooms designed for singles.

Some tour operators, such as such as Intrepid Travel, Road Scholar (formerly Elderhostel) and Holland America Cruise Line, have a roommate matching option. For gay singles, Atlantis Events and RSVP Vacations (primarily for gay men) and Olivia Travel (for lesbians only) have roommate share programs, too.

Another option may be to book at the last minute and ask if they will waive the single supplement. If a cruise or tour still has openings, they would prefer to have one passenger in a room rather than have the room go empty.

Most cruises have special singles mixers. If you're concerned about meeting people on a cruise, make friends before you go on discussion boards for upcoming cruises on CruiseCritic.com. There may be a Facebook group for your upcoming cruise.

There are plenty of alternatives for inexpensive travel, so traveling solo can still be affordable.

Safety can be a concern for a single traveler.

Solo travelers should exercise common sense and follow several safety precautions.

If you're exploring on your own, leave a note with your day's itinerary in your hotel room so that if you don't return, authorities will know where to start looking for you.

Stay in open, public spaces, especially at night.

Research maps, transportation schedules, and prices before you venture outside. If you look like you're lost, you may become a target for unscrupulous people.

Exude confidence and walk purposefully.

Learn how much a taxi should cost and verify the amount with the driver before you begin the ride. Ask the hotel's concierge or front desk staff to summon a reputable taxi for you.

Dress in a manner that will fit in with the locals. Clothing that depicts tourist attractions or other places you have visited will serve to label you as a tourist.

It's a good idea to program the number of the local police into your phone.

On the other hand, as a single traveler you will blend in with a crowd more easily than a group of tourists would.

You may be concerned about whether you will be lonely when you travel solo.

In many destinations, it's easy to strike up a conversation with locals or fellow travelers if you keep yourself open to that possibility. Most waiters, hotel staff, and fellow travelers will be happy to provide recommendations and give advice if asked. If you stay at a bed and breakfast or an Airbnb rental, your host will be accustomed to helping guests find their way around.

Asking someone else to take your picture is a great way to break the ice. When you see a group of people positioning themselves for a photo, you can offer to take their picture for them so that everyone in their party can be in the picture.

You can also use social media to find other solo travelers. Try looking for Meetup groups to find events such as photography walks and happy hours.

Most cities have restaurants or bars that are popular with expats. You should be able to find them online or by asking locals. There, you can meet other English-speaking people who can give you tips or include you in their activities.

Don't assume that younger people won't want to be bothered with older folks. You will find that most people aren't too concerned about age differences. Other cultures respect age in ways that North America doesn't. You are, by the mere fact that you're traveling solo, adventurous and interesting to many.

If you're not sure you are ready to take a major trip by yourself, start by traveling to nearby destinations for a weekend. It you're not ready to travel to another part of the world, start out closer to home by traveling to someplace in the United States, Canada or the United Kingdom, where language won't be a barrier. You don't have to pick a particular spot – sometimes a road trip makes a great adventure.

Most of all, traveling solo builds confidence.

Some people claim that they discover themselves as much as they discover the places they travel to. When you travel with others you will find friendship, diversion and fun. When you travel alone you just might find yourself.

PART SIX

Looking Ahead

Chapter 19

Your Retirement is a Journey, not a Destination

"Nobody grows old merely by living a number of years. We grow old by deserting our ideals. Years may wrinkle the skin, but to give up enthusiasm wrinkles the soul."
- Samuel Ullman

Throughout your working years, you have probably viewed your retirement as a destination. It is a goal you are saving for and will hopefully reach one day. But once you reach this destination, then what?

The perception of retirement as a destination may be why some people approach retirement with dread rather than anticipation. They view retirement as a finish line or as the end of the road.

But retirement is simply a milestone you pass on your journey. It's like crossing the border from one state to the next. The road will continue to unfold before you.

Your life has changed in countless ways from the time you graduated from school and entered the full-time work force until the present. You have probably changed jobs and perhaps changed careers. You may have lived in numerous places, gotten married, and raised a family. Friends have come and gone, your hobbies and interests have evolved, and your body has changed.

Your retirement could easily last two or three decades. It won't be a one-dimensional, stagnant state of being. Your life will continue to evolve in many ways after you retire. You may move, the people in your life will continue to shift, and you will probably travel to new places and engage in new activities.

You may not see your life changing much on a day-to-day basis, just as it didn't seem to change much during your working years. But whenever you stop and reflect back over a year, five years, or ten years, you will be amazed at how much has changed and how your life continues to evolve.

Your retirement journey will probably pass through several phases. They won't be delineated by specific events or ages, but by gradual transitions. The phases will overlap and some will last longer than others.

The go-go years

If you retire in your mid-50s to mid-60s, you will probably still be in reasonably good health and be able to live an active and independent lifestyle. Despite your chronological age, you don't feel old yet. In fact, you're not even sure what "old" is supposed to feel like.

These are the years you will probably fill with traveling, physical activities, and organizations to join. You'll have plenty of time for gardening and home projects, and you may move to a different place to enjoy your retirement. Your schedule may seem as full as it was when you worked, but being busy and active at this stage of your life is good for you both mentally and physically.

The slow-go years

After a while, age will start to catch up to you. You will probably still travel, but your suitcase will seem heavier and your daily itinerary will be lighter. You'll probably favor shorter trips to closer destinations.

While you may not be able to engage in as much physical activity, there's still plenty to do. You can continue to stay mentally engaged by taking classes and enjoying concerts, theatre, and museums. There are still many hobbies and crafts you can enjoy which don't require strenuous activity. You will probably appreciate more time for relaxation.

The no-go years

Ultimately, you will reach a point where you will have to curtail many of the activities you have enjoyed up to this point. You may require some assistance from family members, friends, or hired help, or you may need to move to an assisted living or continuing care facility.

Fortunately, there are still things you can do. You will have more time for reading, enjoying your music or movie collection, or working puzzles. If you like to write, you can create your memoir, document your family history, or write poetry or fiction. With all of today's communication media, it is easier than ever to stay in touch with your family and friends and keep up with what is happening in the world.

Knowing that your retirement will change over the course of many years will raise your awareness of the possibilities you have for the rest of your life.

If you have a long list of things you want to do after you retire, you will be better able to plan for what you should focus on during each phase of your retirement.

On a more philosophical level, you will be able to appreciate the passage of time and the gifts that each phase of your life has to offer.

Chapter 20

How to Turn Your Bucket List into Reality

"To achieve great things, two things are needed; a plan, and not quite enough time."
- Leonard Bernstein

Do you have a bucket list?

If you are not familiar with the term "bucket list," it is a list of things you want to do before you "kick the bucket" (die). It came into common usage as a result of a movie called "The Bucket List," starring Jack Nicholson and Morgan Freeman, which was released in December, 2007. It's remarkable how this term has become so engrained in the American psyche in just ten years.

Having a bucket list is good, but will you actually get around to doing the things on your bucket list? It's easy to get consumed by the routine of day-to-day life, even in retirement. Before you know it, years will have passed and those items on your bucket list will still be just dreams for "someday."

Here are five steps you can take to help you achieve the items on your bucket list and enjoy the fulfilling retirement you deserve.

1. Put it in writing!

Is your bucket list just a vague, ever-changing set of ideas in your head, or do you have yours written down?

Actually writing a list of things you want to do during the remainder of your life will increase the probability that you will achieve them. Plus, you will view your retirement more positively when you have specific things to look forward to.

If you don't have a bucket list in writing yet, grab a pen and paper or open up a new document on your computer. Capture ideas as they occur to you. For now, don't filter yourself.

Your bucket list can contain places you would like to visit, both in your home country and abroad. Perhaps you have projects you wish to undertake, such as cataloging all of your photos or writing your memoir. Consider new things you want to learn and new things you want to try, like taking Spanish lessons or learning how to fly a plane. Think back through your life and try to recall things that once interested you but you never had time for.

You'll probably want to return to writing your bucket list several times in the near future as new ideas come to you.

If you already have a bucket list, get it out. What new things would you like to add? What have you accomplished since you last reviewed your list?

In this chapter, I am going to focus on your travel bucket list – your list of places you want to visit and location-specific things you want to do. Following that, I'll share a few ways you can make your travel dreams easier to achieve.

Think about all the places that you've never been that you would like to visit someday, and add them to your list. Perhaps there are places you visited earlier in your life which you would like to revisit, such as your college campus, the town you grew up in, or a place your family vacationed in your childhood.

The scope of this list is entirely up to you. Regardless of what kinds of travel you prefer or whether you are inclined to stay in your home country or travel the world, your list will reflect your preferences.

For now, don't filter yourself. Don't stop yourself from writing something on the list because you are certain that it would be too expensive and out of your reach. You will edit your list later. For now, let yourself run free with possibilities.

If you are having trouble coming up with ideas, here are 25 suggestions, in no particular order.

- Visit every U.S. National Park. If this seems like too much, just go for major ones such as the Grand Canyon, Yellowstone, and Yosemite.
- Visit Machu Picchu
- Attend a major sporting event, such as the Super Bowl, Kentucky Derby, or Indianapolis 500
- Attend the Rose Parade
- Take a helicopter ride over the Grand Canyon
- Take a European river cruise
- Visit Antarctica
- Watch a baseball game in every major league stadium
- Visit all 50 states
- Take an African photographic safari
- See the Aurora Borealis
- Ride the trans-Canada railway across Canada
- Cruise through the Panama Canal
- Visit the Great Wall of China
- Visit the Galapagos Islands
- Cruise through Milford Sound, New Zealand
- Explore the Louvre
- Visit the Acropolis
- Visit the Pyramids
- Take a coast-to-coast amusement park trip
- Scuba dive in the Great Barrier Reef, Australia
- Take a world cruise
- Visit Niagara Falls
- Visit Iceland

- Visit Tahiti and stay in one of those bungalows over the water

Your travel bucket list items don't have to be exotic or grandiose. Weekend trips to destinations that are within a few hours' drive are perfectly fine.

2. Edit your list

You probably noticed that some of the items you wrote down are rather general (take a European river cruise, visit Iceland), while others are more specific (attend the Rose Parade, take a helicopter ride over the Grand Canyon).

The more specific you can make your bucket list item, the better. For example, rather than listing "Thailand," you can write "take a Thai cooking class in Bangkok" or "visit a Buddhist temple in Chiang Mai." Or, you can write "Thailand," then list the things you would want to see and do there as sub-bullets.

If there are any items on your list that really don't excite you, remove them. If there are things you put on the list because you think you *should* do them, but you don't really *want* to do them, cross them off. And while it's good to be optimistic and think positively, if there are any items on your list that are unrealistic because they are beyond your physical capability or financial reality, delete them.

It's important to believe that everything on your list is achievable, even if it requires a stretch.

3. Prioritize

Choose which item on your bucket list you will accomplish first. Then choose the next five.

If there are items on your bucket list that are more physically demanding and will be easier for you to accomplish while you are younger, you may wish to focus on them first. Climbing Mt.

Kilimanjaro or scuba diving at the Great Barrier Reef might be doable in your early retirement years, but may become more difficult or impossible during your later years.

Since none of us knows how much time we have left, you may prefer to prioritize the items that are most important to you.

If you are married, ask your spouse to write a travel bucket list, then compare and merge your lists.

4. Schedule it

Now comes the fun part. This is the part where the bucket list changes from a wish list to a to-do list. This is where it becomes real.

Pick the date you want to go on your first bucket list trip – even if it's a year or two in the future, and even if the dates are somewhat tentative at this point. Block off those dates on your calendar so that you don't commit to doing other things on those dates.

For the rest of your top five, write down the year you plan to go. If you want to set target dates for more than five, so much the better!

Remember, if you don't write it down and schedule it, it probably won't get done.

When you make the commitment to your next bucket list trip, it's remarkable how everything else falls into place. With your next trip as an established goal, you will find ways to save and prioritize in order to make your trip a reality.

If you can take one bucket list trip a year, you will probably be able to work your way through most, if not all, of the destinations on your list. Even if you don't make it to all of them, you'll accomplish a lot more than you would have otherwise.

5. Identify what it will take to get it done

Those trips on your list aren't going to happen by themselves. Trips take a lot of planning and saving.

Start researching how much it's going to cost. Visit a variety of travel blogs and other websites to learn more about what there is to see and do at your destination.

When you can afford to do so, buy the plane tickets. Make the hotel or cruise reservations. For some destinations such as popular national parks, you have to reserve well in advance. It may take a leap of faith to do this, but it solidifies your commitment to your dreams.

If you currently lack the financial resources to do an item on your bucket list, would you be willing to spend less on other things, such as eating out? Would you be willing to get a job to earn the money?

Some items on your bucket list may require trade-offs. For example, if you want to travel cross-country in an RV, that will require not only purchasing the RV, but also giving up almost all of the other activities and commitments in your life. Will you sell your home, find someone to house-sit or rent it, or simply leave it unattended?

Another reason that some items on your bucket list may never get done is that they require change. They may require you to establish new habits, become more disciplined, or leave your comfort zone. We talked about change in the chapter, "To Enjoy the Retirement of Your Dreams, What Are You Willing to Change?"

*****

Here are four strategies to make your bucket list trips easier to afford.

1. Subscribe to discount travel websites

Sometimes they offer incredible deals.

Be sure to thoroughly read the descriptions of what is included and what is not. Sometimes trips that look inexpensive only include the airfare and lodging, and no excursions or tour guide services are included. Also research your accommodations (both hotels and cruise ships) to ensure that the level of quality and amenities and the hotel's location is satisfactory to you. Bargain travel packages often include lower-rated accommodations or hotels that may be farther away from the tourist zones.

Many discounted packages are cheaper because they take place during the off-season. Research the typical weather patterns for the time of year you will be traveling.

It may be tempting to buy deals that aren't on your bucket list just because they seem cheap. That's OK if you know you will truly enjoy that vacation, but you will be postponing your bucket list dreams.

2. Sign up for a credit card that earns travel miles

You can either acquire a card that is offered by the airline you fly most frequently, or get a bank card that accumulates points that you can exchange for airline miles or hotel stays. Many of these cards offer a large signing bonus of up to 60,000 miles – enough for a trip! You can use this card for all of your everyday spending to accumulate miles, in addition to the miles you earn on trips.

3. Use vacation rental sites such as Airbnb and VRBO to stay in a destination longer and cheaper

Staying in hotels is the most expensive way to travel. Renting a furnished home or apartment is much cheaper, and it's ideal for staying in a place for several weeks in order to truly live like the locals. You can buy food in local stores and prepare it at home, rather than eating all of your meals in restaurants.

4. Volunteer at a National Park

Visiting some or all of the 59 National Parks in the United States is on many people's bucket lists.

Many parks are isolated, so housing is provided for volunteers. Depending on the park, volunteers' accommodations may include fully furnished houses, volunteer villages, seasonal homes, dorms, bunkhouses or RV and camp sites. In exchange for housing, volunteers work at least 20 hours a week.

If you're interested in visiting National Parks but not volunteering, anyone over 62 can purchase a Senior Pass for $80 that will grant you admission to every National Park or Natural Wildlife Refuge for the rest of your life! Only one pass is needed per car. Discounts on camping fees may also be available.

Chapter 21

Will You Be Happy After You Retire?

"Happiness is the experience of loving life.
Being happy is being in love with that momentary experience."
- Robert McPhillips

On its face, this may seem like a rhetorical question. After all, you won't have to work anymore! You will no longer have to deal with pressure, deadlines, performance reviews, demanding customers, or annoying co-workers. You can shut off the alarm clock and get up when you want. And best of all, no more boss! (Well, except maybe your spouse.) Why wouldn't you be happy after you retire?

As it turns out, enjoying a happy retirement does not automatically happen when you kiss the old job goodbye. Not surprisingly, it takes more than simply saving enough money.

While what makes you happy is as individual as you are, these four tips will enable you to make good lifestyle choices and approach retirement with the right frame of mind to truly be happy after you retire.

1. Realize that happiness comes from people and experiences, not things.

For most of your working years, you were probably focused on making money and accumulating possessions. You probably had your sights set on the next thing you wanted to acquire, such as a boat, a bigger house, or a nicer car.

Later in life, you will realize that these things don't really bring happiness. In retirement, you may downsize to a smaller house and share one car with your spouse, while you find happiness in the people you associate with and the activities you engage in. Many people discover that they are happier after they rid their homes and their lives of possessions that no longer hold meaning for them.

It's also erroneous to think that saving more money for retirement automatically equals more happiness in retirement. While it's true that having more financial resources will enable you to do more things you enjoy doing and relieve the stress that comes with struggling to make ends meet, the happiest retirees aren't necessarily the ones who are driving a Mercedes and taking four luxury cruises a year.

Wes Moss, author of *You Can Retire Sooner Than You Think*, surveyed over 1,200 people and found that their level of happiness reached a plateau at about $500,000 in retirement savings. While that is significantly less than most experts recommend that you have in your nest egg when you retire, it illustrates that once basic needs are met, more money by itself does not equal more happiness.

2. Strive for a balance of physical activity, mental stimulation, socialization, and fulfillment.

These are the four pillars of a happy, well-balanced life.

While you may not be able to run marathons, play contact sports, or climb the highest mountains during your later years, activities such as walking, biking, hiking, swimming, tennis, golf, and many other recreational activities will get you out of the house and keep you healthier and happier longer.

Even though you will no longer need continuing education to sustain your career, there's no reason not to continue learning. Many seniors enroll in college courses just to learn about subjects they are interested in. Mental stimulation does not have to take place in a classroom; art museums, history museums, theatre, and concerts provide mental stimulation as well as cultural enrichment.

During your working years, you have people in your life all day long. You might not consider your co-workers to be close friends, but they provide the benefit of human contact. After you retire, most of your work relationships will fade away, so it's up to you to cultivate a network of people you enjoy and take the initiative to spend time with them. It's not difficult to do, but it doesn't happen as easily as it used to. It requires conscientious effort.

Fulfillment means something different for each of us. It may be hard to define, but you know when you feel it. Fulfillment comes from anything that makes you feel happy, alive, and complete. It's whatever makes your heart sing. It's how you feel when you are "in your zone."

3. Discover a new sense of purpose.

A life filled with nothing but pleasure and entertainment will be fun for a while, but sooner or later it will leave you feeling empty and bored. People are happiest when they have purpose and meaning in their lives and they are pursuing their passions or helping others.

If you were heavily absorbed in your career, you might experience a lack of purpose or identity once you leave your career behind. If this happens to you, think back on what interested you earlier in your life – especially during your teenage and college years, or perhaps the years before your children came along. Make a list of the activities you had to set aside because the demands of being a working adult took over. Write down all the things you have ever thought you might like to do "someday."

Once you retire, you will be able to pursue what you are truly passionate about, without concern for whether or not you can earn a good living doing it. You might make your most significant contributions to the world during your retirement!

4. Decide to be happy!

If you are unhappy during your working years, the act of retiring by itself won't turn you into a happy person. In the words of Abraham Lincoln, "Most folks are about as happy as they make up their minds to be." Approaching retirement with a positive attitude makes a big difference.

There's good reason to be optimistic! A recent Merrill Lynch study reported that 93% of retirees said their life is as good as or better than it was prior to retirement. The study characterizes ages 61 to 75 as the retirement "freedom zone," when people enjoy the greatest balance of health, free time, fun, and emotional well-being.

Without the constraints of work, you can choose the activities you wish to pursue, the people you want to associate with, and your attitude. Your retirement offers you a fantastic opportunity to design your life to achieve happiness.

Chapter 22

10 Ways to Stay Young-at-Heart After You Retire

"I will never be an old man. To me, old age is fifteen years older than I am."
- Bernard Baruch

While you have some control over the physical aging process with a healthy diet and moderate exercise, the fact that your body ages as you get older is inevitable. However, you have much greater control over your attitude towards aging.

Since growing older is inevitable, you might as well embrace the experience. Every period of your life has its rewards. Rather than being depressed about the things you can no longer do, celebrate all the things you can still do and the fact that you now have more time to do them.

Here are ten steps you can take to cultivate a positive, youthful attitude at any age.

1. Resurrect youthful passions.

You probably have hobbies or interests that you enjoyed when you were younger but had to put aside when the demands of work and raising a family took over. After you retire, you have the time to enjoy them again or to try new things. Many older people participate in choruses or bands like they did in high school. Others pursue photography, art, writing, crafts, or taking adult education classes.

2. Rid your life of toxic people.

You don't need people in your life who make you feel depressed or bad about yourself. Life is too short! During your working career, you sometimes had to endure the company of co-workers you wouldn't otherwise choose to be around. Now, you have much more choice in the people you spend your time with. Your attitude and your enjoyment of life are heavily influenced by those with whom you associate the most, so find people who are interesting and fun to be around.

3. Stay active.

If you're able, make time in your life for a low-impact sport such as golf, pickleball, biking, swimming, or bowling. Strive to take a 30-minute walk several days a week. Join clubs and go on outings that will give you the opportunity to interact with other people and experience new things. Discover the attractions in your own community such as restaurants, parks, and museums that you may not have had time for during your working years.

4. Maintain a positive attitude.

There may be some things you can't do anymore, so focus on those that you can. Look for the humorous things that happen in everyday life. Don't complain or be resentful; nobody likes to hang around bitter people. Strive to be kind, gracious, and thankful. Although aging is not always easy, remember that it is a privilege that has been denied to some.

5. Make friends with people of different ages.

You might be surprised at how many younger people enjoy the company of older folks. To many people, age is just a number. They are more concerned with your personality, attitude, and common interests. Younger people can bring vitality and fresh perspectives to your life. You may serve as a role model or a source of wisdom and stability for them without even realizing it. If you live in a 55+ active adult community, don't isolate yourself and limit your interactions to other seniors. Venture out and enjoy the rest of the community.

6. Keep up with modern technology.

Become more computer-savvy if you need to. Knowing your way around the internet will enable you to research medical issues, make travel plans, and explore almost any topic that interests you. Most personal business can be transacted online, and you can find information on almost anything. For many people, electronic tools such as text messaging, Facebook and Instagram have replaced letters and telephone calls as their preferred modes of communication. Even email is declining in popularity. If you hope to stay in touch with younger friends and relatives, you'll need to use the communication tools they use.

7. Stay connected with the world.

Familiarize yourself with modern culture. While you may not care much for modern music and entertainment trends, you should still have a passing familiarity with what they are. *Saturday Night Live* is still as funny and relevant as it was in the 70s and 80s. Keep up with current events and get your news from a variety of sources in order to minimize bias and inaccuracies.

8. Don't say whatever comes into your head.

You have probably encountered older folks who seem to think they have earned the right to spout whatever they want, especially when it comes to judgements or critical opinions. You still need filters and decorum. The cranky curmudgeon act gets old fast. Also, be mindful of repeating the same stories and jokes over and over.

9. Don't glorify the past.

It's easy to remember the good times from years past while forgetting about the difficult times you faced. Every decade had its share of corrupt politicians, social injustices, wars, and problems. So stop comparing things to when you were younger. Even if the old days were better, those days are gone. Today is what you have now. Make the most of today.

10. Avoid the "organ recital."

It's OK to mention recent ailments or upcoming operations briefly, but don't make them the focus of your entire conversation. Nothing says "old fart" like constantly dwelling on your aches, pains, and maladies. People will enjoy conversations with you much more when there are many other topics you are able to talk about.

Chapter 23

12 Regrets You Can Avoid in Retirement

"A man is not old until regrets take the place of dreams."
- John Barrymore

Your retirement presents you with the opportunity to truly live your life on your own terms. You are no longer bound by the constraints of your job. You are now free to do the things you have wanted to do for years, limited only by your available resources and your mobility. It would be unfortunate to reach the end of your retirement journey, only to have regrets for the things you could have done, but didn't.

With a little thoughtfulness and planning, you can avoid these twelve regrets during your retirement.

1. Neglecting your health

During your 30s and 40s, you may have picked up some extra pounds and some unhealthy habits. At the time, these issues were easy to ignore and you probably felt like you were getting along fine. But in your 50s and 60s, the years of neglect will take their toll in the form of expensive medical procedures, decreased mobility, and a reduced life expectancy, all of which will result in a shortened, more constrained retirement. Make sure this doesn't happen to you by including some physical activity in your routine. Get regular exams, screenings, dental checkups, and colonoscopies. Monitor your cholesterol, blood pressure, and weight.

2. Not traveling when you had the chance

If travel is a significant part of your retirement plans, don't postpone your dream trips too long. You never know when your health or mobility will start to decline. In the worst case scenario, you or your spouse could pass away unexpectedly. Aim to take your most eagerly anticipated trips within the first few years of retiring. If you remain healthy longer than that, so much the better. Just be careful not to overspend during your first few years of retirement. It's a delicate balancing act.

3. Working too long

If you are approaching retirement with inadequate savings, working a few more years might be a necessity. But many people work longer than they need to, either because they are afraid that they will be miserable after they retire or because they may not realize that they have sufficient resources to retire. Working too long is one of the most common regrets of people who are approaching the end of their life. People rarely regret that they didn't work longer.

4. Not planning for how you will spend your time

During your working years, much of your schedule and your priorities were dictated by your job and the requirements of raising a family and maintaining a home. Suddenly finding that you are completely in control of how you spend your time might be a major adjustment. Retirement brings endless possibilities for things to do, but you need to think about what will be most satisfying to you and take the initiative to create a lifestyle that you will enjoy. Ideally, that will include a mix of physical activity, social contact, mental stimulation, and fulfillment.

5. Not downsizing earlier

While it may be difficult and time-consuming to part with possessions you have accumulated over your lifetime, when you finally do get rid of things you no longer need it will feel liberating. Most retirees who declutter their lives wish they had done it sooner. Many also come to the realization that they wish they hadn't bought most of that stuff in the first place. Moving to a smaller house may be advantageous as well. You'll have a smaller house to maintain and the proceeds from the sale of your larger house may give you more funds to enjoy your retirement.

6. Moving without doing thorough research

If you dream of moving after you retire to a place that is less expensive or features a climate that is more to your liking, be sure to thoroughly research your intended destination before you make the big move. Take several extended trips to the area you are considering at different times of the year, or better yet, rent a home for at least half a year before you totally commit. Favorite vacation destinations rarely make good choices for permanent day-to-day living.

7. Not becoming more financially astute

While you may not acquire as much knowledge as a professional financial advisor, it is beneficial to have a working knowledge of investment products and terminology. You will be in a better position to understand your options and make the best choices for your needs. Many people approach retirement without a full understanding of how Social Security and Medicare work, how much they will need to live on, and how much they can safely withdraw each year. You don't want to make costly mistakes you will regret later.

8. Not getting professional advice

Even if you are a reasonably astute investor, a financial adviser will probably be able to suggest investment options you might not be aware of that will help you save more money for retirement. He or she will have better insight into matters such as tax consequences and how much money you can safely withdraw after you retire.

9. Not creating an estate plan

It may be uncomfortable to think about what is going to happen to your remaining money and possessions after you are gone, but you'll enjoy peace of mind after you create an estate plan. It's tempting to put off this task for another day, but none of us knows how much time we have left. Creating a good estate plan is also a gift you are giving to your beneficiaries, because settling your estate will be faster and easier for them.

10. Not telling people you love them or how much they matter

Sadly, as you get older you will lose more of your friends and family members. Don't wait until it's time to deliver a eulogy or send a sympathy card to express how much someone meant to you. Tell them while they are still alive. Think of how wonderful it feels when someone tells you what a difference you have made in their life. Give that gift to others before it's too late.

11. Carrying grudges

Life is too short. The time you spend focused on holding grudges is time you are depriving yourself of happiness. Make peace with people you would like to be on better terms with. Forgive people who have wronged you. Let go of disappointments, missed opportunities, and past failures. As the ancient wisdom goes, when you hold onto a piece of hot coal with the intent of throwing it at someone else, you are the one who gets burned.

12. Not spending enough time with those you love

After you leave work, you won't be surrounded by people on a day-to-day basis. You will have more time to spend with people, but you'll find that you need to take more initiative to make that happen. It's worthwhile to do so. Make the effort to stay in touch with your friends and spend time with them. If your parents and older relatives are still alive, visit them and ask them to tell you stories about their lives. You will find that your relationships and experiences are the most valuable things in your life.

About the Author

Dave Hughes is a leading authority on retirement lifestyle planning. He writes about retirement lifestyle planning on his website, RetireFabulously.com and in his previous book, *Design Your Dream Retirement: How to Envision, Plan For, and Enjoy the Best Retirement Possible.*

In 2016-2017, Dave was a regular contributor to U.S. News' *On Retirement* blog. In 2017, RetireFabulously.com received the Best Senior Living Award from SeniorHomes.com as one of the top retirement blogs, by both reader polling and judge's selection. Dave was named one of NextAvenue.com's Top 50 Influencers in Aging for 2017.

Following a successful 34-year career as a software engineer, trainer and course developer, and manager, Dave accepted an early retirement package and retired at age 56.

During the final phase of his working career Dave started searching the internet for information about what life in retirement is really like. He discovered that at least 95% of all the retirement-related information was focused on the financial aspects of retirement – how much money you'll need, how you should shift your investment mix as you get older, how fast you can draw down your savings, and so on. Relatively little was being written about how to live a happy, fulfilling life during retirement, and of that, practically nothing was being written from an LGBT perspective.

Dave created RetireFabulously.com to fill that void. Dave has extensively researched retirement lifestyle issues, as well as drawing upon his own experiences of transitioning into retirement and those of others.

Dave is an accomplished public speaker and workshop leader. He was active in Toastmasters International for over eight years, and has earned Distinguished Toastmaster, that organization's highest honor. Dave offers a fun and engaging workshop, also called *Retire Fabulously!*, that brings to life many of the key messages that he presents on his website and in this book.

In addition to writing articles for RetireFabulously.com and books about retirement lifestyle planning, Dave is a wedding officiant and a jazz trombonist. Dave lives in the suburbs of Phoenix, Arizona with his husband Jeff and two dogs, Missy and Maynard.

Dave is available for interviews, speaking engagements, workshops, panel discussions, and writing guest articles. You may contact Dave at SSIR-book@retirefabulously.com.

Please visit these websites to learn more:

RetireFabulously.com

TheDaveHughes.com

Made in the USA
Columbia, SC
29 June 2019